DAYBREAK

A Christian Anthology

by

Terri A. Goins

Order this book online at www.trafford.com
or email orders@trafford.com

Most Trafford titles are also available at major online book retailers.

Printed in Victoria, BC, Canada.

ISBN: 978-1-4269-3066-9 (sc)

ISBN: 978-1-4269-3067-6 (hc)

Library of Congress Control Number: 2010904146

*Our mission is to efficiently provide the world's finest, most comprehensive book publishing
service, enabling every author to experience success. To find out how to publish your book, your
way, and have it available worldwide, visit us online at www.trafford.com*

Trafford rev. 7/26/2010

 www.trafford.com

North America & international
toll-free: 1 888 232 4444 (USA & Canada)
phone: 250 383 6864 ♦ fax: 812 355 4082

DAYBREAK – INDEX

Preface

I believe it is essential that you, the reader understand I write with a prophetic voice of inspiration regarding this endeavor. I am not so special compared with other human beings, as we each bring unique gifts and callings all originating from God's divine plan. I thoroughly believe the realm I seek is available in some form to anyone seeking the face of God. I reiterate, I have done nothing for this privilege. It seems as though this is just one of those things for which God called me. I have however, spent much time in prayer, asking, seeking, and surrendering to Him as much as I know how with a desire to be obedient with a contrite heart towards my Father. I am not and shall never be perfect in the human sense of the word. I blunder, trip and fall like any other child learning to walk. In this journey, I have learned to better listen to the sweet Holy Spirit beckoning my soul to know when and how I error, then accept His guidance and instruction to move forward. With this leading, I have learned I can put anything behind me without reservation and overcome.

Jesus is my Navigator, my God – my Captain, the Holy Spirit – my Lighthouse, and I – the helmsman of the ship passing through this sea of life. I am only the helmsman. The Navigator reports to the Captain and I follow the orders He passes on. To fail to follow orders leads the ship I steer off course and discredits my usefulness to the Captain of the vessel. I am not my own. I serve in obedience under higher authorities. I have been bought with the price of perfect obedience through the blood of Jesus Christ, my Savior. The peace our God grants assures me that my path involves angelic messengers and protection. Life is full of rocks near rocky shores that we steer clear of at times and wreck on at others. I rely on the Navigator to actively search for the beacon's light to protect the vessel in regard to temptations and life's challenges. I strive to hear and obey only the Captain's voice. I am not and will never be the Captain in the sense that God is. I am a helmsman and a masterful one I will become –one order at a time.

I dedicate these pieces to Almighty God and entrust them to you the reader with the hope they will speak to your life's passage and bring you comfort, encouragement, and direction; but most of all convince or assure you that the grace of God is sufficient to meet all your needs.

To my parents -- I wish you a Happy 50th Anniversary. Thanks for providing a loving and stable home throughout the years. To my best friend Sandy, I thank you for years of a kind listening ear, for being and allowing me to be real, and all of your encouragement. To my husband, I thank you for the patience and confidence in us that allows me to pursue my dreams. A special thanks to my proofreaders: Mom (Ann Davis), Sandy James, Lewis and Vivian Talmadge, Rita Boggess, and Beverly Arwood. Your time, effort, and support are greatly appreciated. For each of you and all the readers, I ask God to continue to bless your lives and bring a greater revelation of how He envelops you in His love. Fair Winds and Following Seas.

ABC's of Christianity

A – abide
B – believe
C – compassion
D – diligence
E – encourage
F – forgiving
G – grateful
H – honest
I – imitator of Christ
J – joyful
K – kindness
L – loving
M – merciful
N – new creation
O – overcomer
P – patient
Q – quickened
R – redeemed
S – Spirit-filled
T – travailing
U – united
V – victorious
W – worshipper
X – Christ (Greek)
Y – yielding
Z – zealous

A Child's Cry

Meditations: Psalms 55:16-17, 22; 61:1-3; 142; Matthew 11:28-30

In the year of the great flood, my languid soul lives in continuous drought. Each moment a test of my strength that is abating with each passing day. The weight of my responsibilities overwhelms me…I am a beached whale, a harvested corn stalk, stagnant water…strength and confidence quickly fading. I think of the future and see dry days in my soul and ponder where I will find the courage to face tomorrow. I don't worry about winning the race anymore, I will consider it a victory only to finish.

I long to see the face of God. I plead for mercy and the indwelling of His Spirit…for cleansing with refining fire. Only He can fill the emptiness in my soul. I recall days past when I would approach His throne as a child, fascinated and trusting of His power. I remember well how He watched over me and assured me of His presence. I recollect how in His presence and security I forsook Him, denied Him, and sought out prodigal ways. And yet, when I thought I was far from Him, He was near, ready to accept my prayer of repentance should I have decided to turn from my ungodliness.

I have waited too long Father, hear my prayer. I cry to You from my inner most being! Protect me from the evils I do not discern or understand. Advise me of Your paths. Call my senses to the attention of Your way. Restore Your righteousness and peace within me. Comfort and protect me in the hour of temptation and despair, lest I lose hope and be swept away by the roaring storms of damning fire that rage to consume me when embers attack. Only in Your arms can my soul find rest.

2

A Child's Restoration

Meditation: Proverbs 9:10; II Chronicles 7:14; Matthew 5:3-12

Father, today I confess my sins to You and I cry out for Your mercy. I have no right, no worthiness in or of myself to ask this of You. I bow to Your Holiness and acknowledge Your supremacy. There is no one else to save me Lord, I myself am inadequate for this task. No other knows me as I am known. No other knew me before I was. No one else will know me after I am not. I pray to You Father, not as the God of my understanding, because that would limit Your power and strength to human understanding. Instead Lord, I pray to You as You are…as You know Yourself to be. I confess my wrongs, my sins to You, because they have held me captive and kept me from seeing Your face and pursuing Your work. Never before have I felt or seen the vileness of my nature…the fallen man within as I now see. I acknowledge my sin as my own feeble attempt to control my destiny and gain equality with You. For such sedition, I stand guilty of high treason – yet, You spare my life. Cleanse me as only You are able. Protect my heart with Your sword and shield – for the evil one hovers above like a vulture. Heal my heart of its unbelief. Restore within my soul the trust and faith as of a child.

A Lot More Than Friendship,
A Little Less Than Love

Father I confess
When I look within my heart
I see a cold and stony place
Without much peace or love
But I just can't seem to change it
And I admit, it will need Your touch.

When I look at Your Son
Who died so unselfishly
I know when I stand
Next to His deeds,
I love a lot more than friendship
But a little less than love
Yes a lot more than friendship
But indeed less than Your love.

So take this stony heart of mine
Cast it into the sea
I don't ever want it found
Tugging within and holding me down
I bow before You now on bended knee and wait
For You to create the loving heart I need.

Father, thank you for changing me
With Your love and power
I shall forever praise Thee
My deliverer and high tower
For Your grace and truth changed me into
One who could love so much more like You.

When I look at Your Son
Who loved so unselfishly
I know when I stand
Next to His deeds,
I love a lot more than friendship
And desire to be more like You
Yes, a lot more than friendship
And desire to be more like You.

Accessing the Power

Scripture References:

Genesis 1-3

Matthew 16:18	I Corinthians 13:12-13
Mark 8:29-36	Ephesians 1:4
Luke 9:20-27	Colossians 1:27; 2:6; 3:3-4
John 14:12; 15:4-5, 14-21	I Thessalonians 5:17
Acts 17:28	Hebrews 5:14; 10:16
Romans 7:14-25	I Peter 1:3; 2:5b; 5:8

How careful am I with my words? Do I ever say things to or about myself or others that I would never utter in a prayer? Would I ever pray curses, destruction, or doubt? Of course not. But, do I ever speak these things? Don't we all? Intentionally or unintentionally, God forgive us, we all do. So my question is this… are my words directed to or about myself or others, any less important than words I direct to God in prayer? Is it possible that all of my words are "prayer" as in communication with either God or the evil one? Could this mean that all of my thoughts, speech, and actions either reflect faith or lack thereof?

First consider the qualities of God: omnipotent and omnipresent. OMNIPOTENT means: all powerful, almighty, sovereign, supreme, unrestricted, unconstrained, divine, unlimited, unlimited in power, all-knowing, boundless, eternal, ruling, reigning, paramount, preeminent, uppermost, superior, most excellent, absolute, greatest, ultimate, exquisite, infinite and vast. OMNIPRESENT means: ubiquitous, universal, all over, everywhere, present, prevalent, pervasive, predominant, prevailing, endless, unfathomable, illimitable, interminable, unbounded, continual, ceaseless, constant, unending, and preponderant.

Now with such qualities, it stands to reason that all of my inner and inter communication is always in His presence whether I desire it or not. So why when my words are always before God would I speak carelessly these words of cursing, destruction, or doubt? Why? Because so often I simply fail to acknowledge or remember the importance of such in the spiritual realm. We humans are so easily misled to living in the immediate here and now with no thought of consequences or failing to realize at the time good or harm in our words. We've all experienced this. When someone says something unkind on purpose. When someone says something ugly without thinking or even giving it a thought of how deeply it could hurt. And how many times have we said words we didn't intend to say that just kind of slipped out or that we didn't intend for certain people to hear (or get wind of)? Bottom line…too many times. And why? Because we were either insensitive or just not thinking. The truth is that in the physical realm, sometimes we get away with our insensitivity or thoughtlessness, because the other humans we are communicating with are the same way. But do we ever escape the effect in the spiritual realm? I don't think so. Perhaps this is why our words can come back and haunt us or convict us. Our words act to hinder our "intentional" prayers and bring us condemnation from the evil one or develop indifference in our spirit and soul affecting our future words. On a positive note, even our accidental or casual words can encourage and bless in the same way.

Scripture says we are to pray without ceasing. I have to wonder how much of the power of God would manifest if we enacted the faith of mustard seed to make sure that all of our spoken words and then our thoughts lined up with the Word of God? Just think of the potential of experiencing God's manifestations and glory now!! Is this possible? Remember Paul's teaching… "Christ in us the hope of Glory"? Too often I'm afraid we only think of Glory as being in the presence of God in the afterlife of Heaven… our experiencing God face to face without physical constraints of time and understanding. I wonder if we could experience more of this Glory and power of our God by watching our words carefully?

Additional Verses to:

A Mighty Fortress is Our God
(Verses 1-4: Martin Luther 1529)

Verse 5:
The Lord Almighty is with us
The God of Jacob our strength
For You have sent the Paraclete
To indwell us and reign.
By Your favor we are blest
And overcome the test
The evil one doth throw,
At us who love You so,
Yet we await Your rapture.

Verse 6:
Holy, Holy is our God
Who's seated in the Heavens
No greater love could He have shown
Than dying for our sins.
May my life reflect
The glory of His presence.
In Heaven He's prepared
A place for those who turn their ear
To the trump of His returning.

Additional Verses to:

And Can It Be?

(Original Words Verses 1-4: Charles Wesley, 1718)
(Music: Thomas Campbell, 1825)

Verse 5:
Look at the Lamb of God
Who takes away the sins of the world!
My debt He cancelled and now I'm free;
What greater love could He have shown me?
Unselfish gift full of love divine
You're my strength and my refuge
My hope, my life!
[Refrain]
Unselfish gift full of love divine
You are my strength, refuge, hope, my life!

Additional Verses to:

<u>Are You Washed in the Blood?</u>

Revelation 7:14 – "These are they who...have washed their robes and made them white in the blood of the Lamb."

(Original words and music verses 1-4)
(Elisha A. Hoffman, 1878)

Verse 5:
No more blood of lambs or bulls and goats
Are you washed in the blood of the Lamb?
Jesus is our sacrifice today
Are you washed in the blood of the Lamb?

Verse 6:
He is our advocate at God's right hand
Are you washed in the blood of the Lamb?
Interceding for His saints right now
Are you washed in the blood of the Lamb?

Verse 7:
He's returning for His Church someday
Are you washed in the blood of the Lamb?
And we shall meet Him in the air
Are you washed in the blood of the Lamb?

Additional Verses to:

<u>Come, Thou Fount of Every Blessing</u>
(Original Verses 1-3: Robert Robinson 1758)

Verse 4:
Every good and perfect gift
Comes from God on High;
Provisions exceeding
From an overflowing supply.
I will praise Thee with my heart
From Your abundance my mouth speaks.
Honor and lauds of glory
To Him in whom I confide.

Verse 5:
I sing glory, hallelujah
Glory be to Him Amen
The Alpha and Omega
Beginning and the End!
Jehovah Jireh, my provider,
El Shaddai, Yahweh,
Father, Son and Holy Spirit
Glory to the Three in One!

Additional Verses to:

<u>Covered by the Blood</u>
(Original Verses 1-4: Nellie Edwards, 20th C)
(Music: Ran C. Story, 20th C)

1. After saving my soul and giving new life
   He did not stop blessing me
   But sent the Holy Spirit, comfort of my soul
   And He keeps my sins under the blood.

2. Now I come boldly to the throne of grace
   For Jesus is there interceding
   And when my God looks at me
   He sees not under the blood.

3. Brother go share the message of Jesus Christ
   Take it to every people, tribe and tongue
   For this He died that by His grace
   All sin would be covered by the blood.

Additional Verses to:

I Would Not Be Denied
{Original verses by Charles P. Jones 1900}

1. In the beginning God created
   The heavens and the earth
   And formed man in His image
   Right from the dirt

Chorus:
He would not let them be denied
He would not let them be denied
In His image God created man
And they would not be denied

2. And when in the Garden
   Satan deceived Eve
   God told of a day to come
   When Jesus would set men free

Chorus:
He would not let them be denied
He would not let them be denied
In His image God created man
And they would not be denied

3. In the days of Old God lived with man
   In the Ark of the Covenant
   And forgiveness came from sacrifices
   On the day of Atonement

Chorus:
He would not let them be denied
He would not let them be denied
Until the Messiah came
He would not let them be denied

4. Jesus was born to us a babe
   In the town of Bethlehem
   Both Son of God and Son of Man
   He came to die for our sins

Chorus:
He would not let them be denied
He would not let them be denied
In His image God created man
And they would not be denied

5. Then one day there was a cry
   From John in the wilderness
   "Make straight your paths
   For the Kingdom is at hand!"

Chorus:
He would not let them be denied
He would not let them be denied
In His image God created man
And they would not be denied

6. Three days in the grave
   They thought Jesus dead and gone
   But glory be, He rose again
   And ascended to the throne!

Chorus:
And we would not be denied
And we would not be denied
For Jesus came to save mankind
So we would not be denied

7. To fulfill man's greatest need
   He sent the Comforter
   Who seals us with the Lamb of God
   And brings joy to our heart!

Chorus:
I will not be denied
I will not be denied
Jesus has come and made me whole
And I will not be denied

8. Satan will try any way he can
   To keep me from my Lord
   So I fervently pray each day
   For God to wield my sword.

Chorus:
I will not be denied
I will not be denied
Jesus has come and made me whole
And I will not be denied

9. Because of God's grace and love
   For my unworthy soul
   Forever I will praise His name
   For making me whole.

Chorus:
I will not be denied
I will not be denied
Jesus has come and made me whole
And I will not be denied

10. The Lord is true to His Word
    He's never told a lie
    So I will trust in Him henceforth
    Until the day I die!

Because I am not denied
Because I am not denied
Jesus has come and made me whole
And I am not denied

11. Dear Jesus cut the strings from my feet
    That to this earth doth bind
    Place that heavenly vision in front of me
    And give me wings to fly!

Chorus:
Because I am not denied
Because I am not denied
In Heaven I'll see His shining face
Because I am not denied.

12. Holy, Holy, Holy
    Is the Lord God Almighty
    Who Was and Is and Is to come
    Hallelujah and Amen!

Chorus:
For I am not denied
For I am not denied
Glory be to Jesus Christ
For I am not denied.

Additional Verses to:

Joyful, Joyful We Adore Thee
(Original Verses: Beethoven 1824)

5. My lips shall ever praise Thee
   Each morning that I arise
   For the beauty You've created
   Both in daylight and at night
   Joyful, joyful, I adore Thee
   Creator of my life
   I lift my voice in honor
   To You eternal God on High!

6. This is my song to You
   Until I meet You in the air
   You are my loving Savior
   Comforter of my every care
   Sender of the Holy Spirit
   Sealing us both here and there
   Accept the praise of your servant
   Lamb of God, hearer of our prayers!

Additional Verses to:

My Savior's Love
(Original verses by Gabriel 1856-1932)

I sought Him in my sin
And yet He received me
I reached my hand for His garment
And His love made me clean.

The angels in glory
Rejoiced in that day
When He extended healing
Broke my chains and set me free!

Now with His ransomed children
His glory at last I see
And forever without ceasing
I'll sing of His love for me.

When the trump shall resound at His coming
Then every man shall know
The love and truth He's spoken
And His promise to return for His own.

Then all will stand amazed in His presence
This Jesus the Nazarene
With knees bowed and tongues confessing
Doubt will no longer be.

Last Chorus:
How Marvelous! How Wonderful
Shall be heard from sea to sea
How Marvelous! How Wonderful
Is my Savior's love for me!!

There is a Fountain

Zechariah 13:1 – "A fountain will be opened…to cleanse
them from sin and impurity."

(Original Words: William Cowper, 1771)
(Music: Traditional American Melody; arr. By Lowell Mason, 1830)

No greater gift is there than this, dying for a friend.
And yet Jesus died for me, though I grieved Him in my sin.
Though I grieved Him in my sin, though I grieved Him in my sin,
And yet Jesus died for me, though I grieved Him in my sin.

Even now I hear the angels sing, Praises to my Lord,
For the love He showed all mankind, dying once and forevermore.
Dying once and forevermore, dying once and forevermore,
For the love He showed all mankind, dying once and forevermore.

Holy, Holy the angels sing around the throne of God;
Worthy of Honor and Praise, I long to sing with them above.
I long to sing with them above, I long to sing with them above.
Worthy of Honor and Praise, I long to sing with them above

And on that day we gather in Heaven and see our name written there,
No greater glory shall await, than to see Him there.
Than to see Him there, than to see Him there,
No greater glory shall await, than to see Him there.

Hallelujah, glory to our God, our King, Emmanuel,
His praises shall I sing eternally, to Him who saved my soul.
To Him who saved my soul, to Him who saved my soul,
His praises shall I sing eternally, to Him who saved my soul.

Additional Verse to:

<u>To God Be the Glory</u>
{Original Verses 1-3: Fanny Crosby – 1875}

4. To God be the glory, great things He hath done
   Planted in His garden and nourished by the Son
   A young plant so tender needing weeded to grow
   Ever reaching skyward, a harvest it holds.

   Chorus:
   Praise the Lord
   Praise the Lord
   Let the earth hear His voice
   Praise the Lord
   Praise the Lord
   Let the soil rejoice
   All come to the Garden
   To be sown in the Son
   Nourished and watered
   'Til the harvest is done.

Additional verse to:

<u>When the Roll is Called Up Yonder</u>
{Original verses 1-3: James M. Black – 1892}

4. So let us proclaim the good news of God,
   Grace for every one,
   That takes away our debts from the face of God.
   Let us shout the news throughout all the lands,
   So when the roll is called up yonder
       they'll be there.

Adoration

O God, my Father
Creator of time
Holy Spirit
Comforter of the Vine
Jesus, Savior, Bridegroom
With You I long to dine
I am Your branch
Grafted into Your vine
Your sap is my strength
My food divine
Redeemer, Renewer
Of my mind
None ever sweeter
Or so kind
Creator Savior
Love of mine
None ever sweeter
Or so kind
Pure love and beauty
In me abide
None ever sweeter
Or so kind
Triune Holy God
I am Thine.

Altar Call

The preacher said:

Your heart can be hardened
on bended knee
Even as you sit in a pew
Comfortably
Each, Sunday and Wednesday eve.
How do I know if your heart's grown cold?
You do not hear
You do not see
You know not the Lord's voice
When He beckons thee.
Life will lose its meaning
And purpose divine
So that you'll go through the motions
With robotic design
And though you don't hear
By this you will know
Your words and deeds
Just will not show.
Although yourself, you may deceive
You won't fool those
In whom God flows.
Life will flow in the redeemed
Those that know the truth
Who are set free...
Who hear His sweet Spirit speak
Yielding fully surrendered
Bowing at His feet.

Here at His altar
The saints kneel in prayer
Calling for repentance and grace
For sinners and saints everywhere
And those prayers for you rise
As an incense from a pleasing sacrifice
Asking forbearance until you defeat the foe
And meet the Lord
At the place you won't yet go.

The preacher is speaking:
This is the altar call
If you desire a Savior
Or need a lift from a fall
No matter what your need
Jesus waits to answer the call
At this very place
Jesus is reaching to you
With His nail scarred hands
He is the conqueror,
Your Healer
Your Friend.

Arise

Arise – Arise
Child of God
There's so much work
to be done in the vineyards
Come join the fun
Harvest the fruit for the Holy One.

Brothers and sisters in unity
A pleasing incense will rise
To His throne on High
As we obey Him.
Can you hear the vineyard's cry?
Waste no time in gathering.

Come now
Come quickly
To honor and praise
The Holy One
Stain your hands
With the fruit of grace
Until you can never
Be the same.

Strengthen our bodies
Restore our sight
To Your vision
Touch our ears
So we can hear
How to proclaim
Your salvation.

Jesus Christ
Son of God
Holy One
We praise You
O precious Lord
Lamb of God.

<u>Ascension</u>

{Psalm 25; Ps. 45:6,7; Isaiah 6:1; Isaiah 66:1;
Hebrews 1:8; Revelation 3:21}

To You, O Lord
I lift my soul
O my God
I trust in You.
I will not be ashamed
Because I've set my eyes
On Your throne of grace.

Your throne of grace
Is forever and ever
Your righteousness
Anoints and heals as oil
Heaven is Your throne
The earth, Your footstool
And yet you bid me to come.

Show me Your ways
Teach me Your statutes
Lead me in Your Truth
And Teach me to hold fast
In the face of men and other gods.
For You are the God
Of my salvation
On You, I wait with expectation.

I remember Your tender mercies
And Your loving kindness
Is forevermore
You convict the sinner and saint alike
And pardon iniquity
So we are righteous
In Your sight.

Who have we
But You, O God?
Surely none is greater
In love or might.
We praise You.

Ask and It Will

{Isaiah 54:17; Matt 7:7-8, 8:13}
{Hebrews 10:23; I John 5:14}

I walked in need
Unable to believe
That God would hear my cries
I knew that He could
But didn't believe He would
Until He asked,
"Why do you fear to receive?
Why won't you ask of me?
Why don't you seek me?
Why haven't you knocked on my door?
Where is your faith?"

Ask and it will
Be given to you
Seek and you will find
Knock and the door will be opened
All who ask receive
All who seek will find
And those who knock
See doors opened unto them.

Then I said to Jesus
With my head bowed low
"Please forgive my unbelief."
Just then He answered,
"Go your way
And as you have believed,
It be so."

I then asked of Him
as He taught me
In His Holy Word
I sought His ways and listened for

His small peaceful voice
I knocked on doors
And beheld their opening
And as I did these, I knew
His Words turned true.

Ask and it will
Be given to you
Seek and you will find
Knock and the door, it will be opened
All who ask receive
All who seek, find
And those who knock
See doors opened unto their eyes.

Do not fear asking
He's the Mighty One
The very provision
For your every need
Seek according to His will
Pray in one spirit to God
Believe your prayers in your heart.

What have you asked of God?
What have you sought Him for?
Have you ever dared to knock on
Kingdom doors?
Have you ever listened and heard His voice?
It is He not I who says….

"Why don't you ask of me?
Why don't you seek me?
Why haven't you knocked on my door?
Don't you know I'm waiting for thee?"

Ask and it will
Be given to you
Seek and you will find
Knock and the door will be opened
Only say the Word
All who ask of Jesus receive
All who seek Him find
All those who knock upon His door
Will enter in His home
And He in their heart.

Assurance

This I ask in intercession
For this temporal house
My living sacrifice
I lift up to You
For I know the thoughts
You have toward man
Of peace
Not evil
For a future and a hope
For us to seek You
With all our heart
Then the angel spoke
Softly in my ear
"O man of dust
do not fear
Jehovah Shammah
He is here."

Authority

Satan would say to me:
"Why waste your time in prayer
surely you're too intelligent
to believe God is really there.
It's just a figment of imagination
passed from age to age.
Man's feeble attempt to understand
what he cannot explain."
And I answered:
"On the Word of God I take my stand.
You father of lies;
your deception cannot prevail.
Darkness vanishes in Light.
The Lord Jehovah delivered authority
And through that power in Jesus Christ
I cast you out.
You must leave."
Lucifer replied:
"Don't waste my time with your Jesus words.
You don't expect me to believe
Jesus can reside in you,
just look at your life!
Don't you remember when…"

And he planted doubts as wild weeds
And all the guilt and shame
flashed before me.

"Tell me how could He indwell a vessel
that's so obviously unclean it's profane?"

And once again I answered:
Now with BOLD authority:
"Satan, your assaults are crafty
but I've been redeemed
My mind renewed by the Spirit
overflowing in me.

I stand against you and praise my God and King
hands raised and voice ascending
for the sacrifice made complete.
Your lies are devoid of power
you cannot prevail
For not I, but the Lord Almighty
Seized the wind from your sails!!"

Battle Cry

I banished you from my presence
And you invaded my dreams.
I resisted your temptations
Refused to worship you
And you took away everything.

In shock, I stood in silence
Unable to comprehend
The destruction before my eyes.
Bombs whistling, grenades exploding,
And shrapnel shredding
With the element of surprise.

And in that battlefield
My spirit cried out to my God
In words beyond my knowing
Though I know not how
I knew I wouldn't die.

And in that wasteland at noonday
My God drew His sword and wielded it before me
And His Kingdom marched on
As shrapnel flew without piercing
Because of the Lord's armor for His saints.

Yes, the Lord protects His own.
His children, He never leaves.
He surrounds them with a shield,
Empowers with His strength
And covers with His anointing.

My God proclaims Victory
Before we ever begin.
O set our eyes on You, Lord
And as in days of Old
Let Your trump resound again.

Be It Unto You
{Matthew 8:5-10}

The soldier came to Jesus saying:
"Master, my servant will You heal?"
"Yes, I will," He answered,
"Lead me to him now."
But the soldier replied:
"Lord, I am not worthy
For you to come into my home.
And I know You need only
Say a word
And it will be done."

And Jesus said:

"Be it unto you
Just as you have believed
Never in all of Israel
Such great faith have I seen
Now go your way
And as you have believed
It will be done for you."
And the servant was healed within the hour.

When I'm faced with trials,
Burdens or cares
So common in this life
Oh help me Jesus, just to trust You
And live my faith
As the soldier did that day.

Before All Men

Before all men let me proclaim
the strong word of the Lord
I will keep silent
only in God's presence
while He speaks to me
Then I will rise
and bring forth His message
to perform His will.

Let the words of the Lord
be written upon my heart
that He may use my hand
while I live
His words will not be hidden
or my mouth silent
lest the rocks begin to cry out.

The mighty Word goes forth
as a sword and discerns
the hearts of men
and never returns void.
O Word of the Lord
guide my ears, heart and hands
my feet, thoughts and my words.

O let this be
all the days of my life
that I may be pleasing to You
on that day I see Your face
All the days, both now and forevermore
Let my voice shout forth
Though bound in shackles
Restrained by chains
Jesus my Lord set me FREE!

Belonging

You are the rock of my salvation
The strength of my life
My only hope and inspiration
Unto You I cry.

Your Word watches over me
And You perform it
You preserve me with
Compassion, love and truth
You are all I've ever needed
Under Your wings, I've found my rest.

The spirit of fear no longer lingers
No longer bound, I'm free
Like a mother with her precious child
My Father delights over me.

<u>Birthright</u>

I am but one grain of salt
in a vast ocean deep
Yet, my Father knows even me.

I am but one grain of sand
on an island in the South Seas
Yet, my Father sees even me.

I am but one speck of dirt
in the farmers harvest field
Yet, my Father knows my worth.

I am but one of human kind
formed from dust by God
Yet, my Father discerns my soul from my mind.

I am but one that will face death
and the judgment of my soul
But when and how I will transcend
from this life to the next
is not my worry
For my Father knows.

Blindness

What O man dost thou know
When in sins sludge thou dost trod?
Art thou deceived so much
That no blindness dost thou see?
For sin shalt gain thee only sin
And greater denial thereof;
Transgression without liberty
By grappling hooks confined.
What greater price shalt thou pay
Than loss of fellowship with thy God?

Buoyancy

Thinking back on my life
Splintered pieces with some misplaced
Others creeping up on me from behind
To this present place.

Days with hopes and dreams
Snatched
Away
Erred patterns of thinking
Poor choices
Apparent to me now
Inflict pain and bring tears flowing
D
O
W
N
As they compete for control of my life
I pray to God above for strength
I seek to live in His powerful grace
Yet feel I'm withering each and every hour
I feel it there deep inside
Striving to overtake from within
That proud and unrepented sin
Battling against serenity.

I cry Please God, no more please!
I'm hurting and am so afraid
I fear the temptation will never cease
And my vigilance will fail
I know without You
I am no more.

Hold me securely in Your loving arms
In tribulation's darkest hour
Deliver me from the Evil One
Who seeks body and soul to devour
In faith I ask Your will be done

On earth as in Heaven it will be
As if Heaven and earth be one.

And when I seek Your face
Let me know You are near
Grant me sight to see Your presence
When all others fear
You've forsaken us
And grant me ears that I might hear
Hear You
Right here where I am
Right here where I am
Let Your light shine brightly within
A beacon near the rocky shore
Right here where I am.

Captain of the Vessel

Help me Lord
To hear Your voice
To distinguish between
Your plans and mine

I am a vessel
That sails on
The waters of Your life
Here one day
And the next one gone

My voyage is Your mission
Not my own agenda
You are the helmsman
I move forward
I turn at your command
Bear right or left
Reverse or stand fast

Grant me Your helmsman's ear
To follow orders in this fog
So I can continue on Your mission
Without delay or loss

I long to be like You, Jesus
Only doing what You
Heard the Father say
An obedient servant
Come wind, hail or rain

Grant to me
The helmsman's ear
So I can steer this vessel
According to Your will
Across the sea of this life
In good repair
No cargo or crew lost
No matter the weather
Cargo stowed securely
With timely re-supply

I desire nothing
But to sail at Your command
On glassy seas or treacherous waves
In light winds or through hurricanes
I am Your vessel
I trust Your hands.

Carnal Mind

Close your eyes to the world you see
Only then will the Master rub spit into your eyes
Loosening the scales that have made you blind
And if you dare see for the very first time
Open again, your God healed eyes.

Catching Away

My spirit rests in full confidence
Of the peace of my God
For the promises He has spoken
I stand and praise my Father

Now watching and waiting
We look to Zion
Knowing and believing
What You said in Your Word

We look to the hills of Zion
For signs of Your return
The day we hear the trumpet
The Eastern skies obey

In that day
In the twinkling of an eye
We'll all be changed
If we heed the warning and seek His face.

<u>Children</u>

Children know
The voice of their parents
Pleasant, comforting
Stern or indifferent
They learn whether arms embrace
Push away
Are absent
Or there to stay
They learn their scent
Natural or perfumed
Smokey or of alcohol
They learn about touch
Soft or muscular
Safe or threatening
Or neglected
They learn of love and hate
Approval and rejection
Satisfaction or disapproval
Success and failure, too
They learn of faces sad or joyful
Confused or confident
Angry or calm
Indifferent or stoic
Not so easily read
And easily confused
They know the face and hands that feed them
Soon after they are born
If they are held close
If they are safe
If they belong
They choose favorite colors
Of the many hues
And develop tastes based on personality and experience
For clothing, music, sports, friends and food

As time passes they grow
And each their own way goes.
But how old do they have to be
To know about You, the Father?
Who is this God our Creator?
When will we put our childishness away
And learn to focus on You?
When will we learn to hear You?
And not just what the world says is true?
When will we ever care
That You love each of us so dear?
When will we put aside
Our pleasurable distractions
To bask in Your embrace?
Do we know Your scent?
If You are near or far away?
Do we seek Your face?
Or walk away indifferent or in fear?
When will we discern Your coming and going away?
When will our yearning to be like You
Be the epic of our faith?

Children's Bread

PRAISE
Our entrance into Your presence
Our corban – access to Your throne
The incense that draws You near.
The weapon of confusion
to our adversary
dense for obscuring
even his familiar path.

Burst forth praise and thanksgiving
Break down man's holy walls
Shout Hosanna in the Highest
From the sun's rise until its fall
Obedience is better than sacrifice
To You I bow with all my crowns.

Choirs of All Creation

I hear the choir of angels singing
Crying out before the Lord
"Holy, holy, holy, holy, holy, holy
Holy, holy, holy
Holy is the Lord over all
May His glory be established everywhere!"

Can you hear the angels singing
As they circle the throne of our King?
"Holy, holy, holy, holy, holy, holy
H-O-L-Y
Holy, Holy, Holy
Is the Lamb."

I hear the choirs of every nation
Bowing down in worship praising
"Glory to the Lord"
And as they sing "Holy Holy"
Incense rises before Him
As He takes a jar and breaks the seal;
Then on His people bowed before Him
He pours out His anointing oil.

Can you hear the healing
Of the bodies, wills and emotions
As He pours out His waterfall of Love?
And I hear Him saying
To the weak and undeserving
"Worthy, worthy, worthy, worthy
Worthy, worthy, worthy, worthy
Worthy is Your Lamb!"

"Come now into My presence
covered by the blood of My Son
You have overcome the enemy
By the blood of My Lamb
And the word of your testimony
Come now and receive your reward.
You are My children
You are righteous
You are Holy
You are worthy
Full of honor
In my image
You are made."

"Now I shall open
more of your spirit
Into the fullness of my Glory;
Forevermore so shall it be
Welcome My child into My Kingdom
Your created destiny."

Church Without Walls

Building with
No roof
To keep the praises from rising
No walls
To keep men out
To form cliques
And segregations
Of superiority
And prejudice.
Souls with
No pretense
In men's hearts
No hypocrisy
Or unforgiveness
Pure exposure
Love in action
To demonstrate the power
Of God.

<u>Come</u>

Meditations: Isaiah 55:8-12, Revelation 22:16-17

I acknowledge Your ways
As higher than my own
Your thoughts are focused
While mine do roam
So my ways
I abandon and leave behind
While I press on
And live in the Mind of Christ.

I receive the Holy Spirit
You sent to witness of yourself
To the churches of past and present
You, the mighty root of David
Very offspring of the eternal God
The radiant start of dusk
And the hope in light of dawn.

The Spirit and the Bride say, "Come."
And let him that hears
Let him too say, "Come."
And let him that is thirsty arise
And whosoever will
Let him drink freely
Of the water of LIFE.

Commission

Lord, I long to be Your disciple
One faithful and true
Doing anything that pleases You.
Show me what it means
To serve you.

So I looked for the hungry
Bought them food
Gave drink to the thirsty
Clothes to the poor
I knew to heal the sick
Cast out evil spirits
Visit those in prison
Go and make disciples
But wondered if there was more.

"Love, like I love," Jesus said to me,
"With forgiveness and compassion
Unconditionally.
Pray to the Father
Do His will
Turn from your sins
Repent and never turn back.
Don't think that your actions
Will ever justify you.
I look not at the outward
But the heart's attitude.
Examine yourself my child,
Cast down vain imaginations
Think only on the good, true, and lovely
And follow Me."

Communion

Come My children
Come to My feast
All is prepared
Come now and eat
The table is spread
I've broken the bread
Fresh wine is poured
Come dine with the Lord.

Confession of a Pharisee

Father help me today to realize
That each man's journey with You
is a personal
private
unique matter.
Abiding in Your truth
I relinquish all my rights
to impose my ways
my beliefs
or my expressions of faith
upon You
or those reaching toward Your light.
Teach Your servant to understand
that my interpretation
of a feeble attempt at reaching towards You
is nothing more or less than my interpretation
my judgment of events and hearts
that I do not fully understand.
Open my heart of understanding to see
that an attempt is an attempt
and You, O Holy God of Israel
are the infallible judge
of feebleness,
attempts,
and humility;
and that even "feeble" attempts
abound in trust and faith
greatly exceeding
no attempt at all.
Forgive this Pharisee
for his blindness and self-righteousness
Transform my ways
that I will not be disqualified
By the testimony of my own words and actions.

Consistency
(Matthew 6:19-21/13:44-46)

I heard the voice behind me say
"Incline thine ear just a bit this way
just one moment please, listen to me."

I questioned turning an ear
to this voice I'd heard
for I feared
in the word evil lurked.
So I kept on walking
Thinking – I will not turn
but my lips were silent
when again I heard…
"Incline thine ear this way please
just a moment of your time.
I've an answer you are seeking.
You'll find it satisfies…"

And just for a moment
the lies I believed
and with those very words
I fell deceived
O that I had hearkened
and never turned an ear
for the voice was a spider
weaving a web of capture
from my drawing near…

"Incline thine ear this way please
just a moment of your time
I've an answer you've been seeking
And it will satisfy…"

Now when I hear these words again
Satan tempts me with shame and defeat
But I refuse to listen
For God swept entangling cobwebs away
He sends the light of His word
forward on my path
The Lord offers a future and hope
and to Him, I've no past.

The Lord my God says
"Let not angry waves toss thee to and fro
I know My sheep by name—
My voice they know.
No sin shall tempt thee
that is not common to man;
And I shall save all
who come to Me and repent."

Conversion

Lord I'm a sinner
And not worthy to pray
But I feel somehow
In some mysterious way
That You love me
Even with my faults.
Being only a man
I cannot comprehend such love
Without You Lord
The stray lambs would be
Forever lost
And the healthy would die
Without guidance.
Only You Lord
Show us the way
The way to Heaven
Prepared by Your name.
Give me strength Lord
To endure what I must
So that I may always
Believe and trust
In Thy Holy Name.
Let my life here
On earth be
A fulfillment of Your will
So be my guide Lord
Your sheep I will be
So my soul lives
Restored and still.

Dawn

Awaken O man
To light of day
Forsake darkness
And sins dead sway
Cries endure but for a night
Then joy comes in the morning.
Arise, O child of the most High
Give glory to the King
The star of salvation's light.
What greater gift canst thou bring
Than the incense of thyself
In God's own image created?

Days of Glory

Lord I've come to worship
And praise Your Holy Name
Forgive and cleanse me
Of all guilt, sin, and shame.
Mighty is Your river
Brilliant is Your light
I worship You in truth
There's no darkness in Your light.

I raise my hands to You, O Lord
No other satisfies
I praise You for opening
My hands, ears, and eyes.
Empower me, Your servant
To go and conquer still
Knowing in You I stand
My lips shall not fail
For Your Glory abounds.

<u>Deception</u>

I've seen friends of mine
Walk away from God for a lie
In the world and of it too
No longer oil floating atop
But their lives as dye mixed in
Blending until no difference can be seen.

<u>Decisions</u>

I know
I will make time
For those things
I treasure in my soul.
So Lord, teach me to make
Teach me to take
More time for You.
Steal me away
From tempting distractions
Cleanse my mind
From the stains of this life.
Purge me with fire
Until I am holy
A pure and spotless
Bride fit for You.

So teach me to make
Teach me to take
More time for You.

Let there be
Nothing more important
Than intimate
Time with You.

Let every step I take
Every breath I breathe
Be with a servant's heart
And the loyalty of a dear friend.

Deliverance Chant

My deliverer has come
My deliverer is at my side
My deliverer has come
I fall on my face in His sight.
My deliverer is my defender
With purifying fire in His eyes.
My deliverer dwells within me
Jesus is my joy, my strength, and my might.
Yes, Jesus is my deliverer
Jehovah has given me life!
I praise Your Name, You are Holy
I exalt Your Name on high.
Highest praise to my deliverer
Who grafted me into His vine.
Glory to my deliverer
Changer of water to wine.
My deliverer is Holy
And He has given me His mind.
My deliverer never changes
His promises of Old are now mine!

Dialogue

Human: I'm better off not seeing You so much right now.
The more I see You, the more I miss You.

Jesus: But pulling away is how relationships die.

Human: I must go. I cannot live torn between two worlds.
I can never measure up to Your expectations.

Jesus: You are right in what you say. You stray. You have already been forgiven if you will receive it. I have already gone ahead and prepared a place for you. I will return again to bring you to where I am and we will never part again. The works I do are not limited to the physical realm, but are able to transform your soul because they are spiritual to the pulling down of strongholds that bind you. Stay with me in this place and follow no voice but mine.

This is a key to how we are to be with Jesus. He should be so close to us, such a part of us, that we miss Him desperately when we're not together. This relationship, this friendship, contains valuable elements regarding the way Christians are supposed to interact because it rises from the foundation of how we're to be with Jesus. Responsibility, accountability, encouragement, and espirit de corps combats depression, fear, and desires of quitting. War either strengthens you and increases your dedication or drives you away in fear. Empty your mold of fear and embrace faith with reliance on the Holy Spirit. What you cannot do, He already has.

Disciple's Song

I've lived my life wondering
Why happiness never lasts
The flowers that bloom in spring
Die when summer is past
The morning sun that rises
Always at dusk doth set
And I sit in darkness wondering
Why happiness never lasts.

I used to believe in silver linings
And fighting to see things through
But recently, with dreams shattered
Now think I'm a fool
What life once seemed so full of hope
Now fades as morning dew
And I wander around looking as though blind
For that which was left behind.

"Stand, watch and pray", He said to me
And I said OK
Though my intentions were true to follow through
I fell asleep and left Him all alone
Did you hear my cry at the cross that dark day
You've been a good friend
I've no doubt you tried your best
But as for me, I'm sinking in the sand
Where happiness never lasts.

As days past, Judas could not stand
The emptiness that engulfed his soul
His joy gone, and his Master, too
The silver marked the betrayal
He took his own life that stung with pain
Thirty pieces of silver and nothing to gain
And the light of day,
Nothing but a dark stormy night
Drenching his weary soul
As the onlookers sat in the darkness full of scorn
Asked if happiness ever lasts.
But then the third day
Mary returned shouting
"He is alive!!
The Jesus that we buried
Is no longer there
And the angel said to pass the word
That HE IS RISEN FROM THE DEAD!"
"Come see here, is this not where He was lain?
Now go to Galilee and He shall meet you there."

O the gloom of days past
No longer holds pain
Since now we understand His plan
Life beyond the grave
The Comforter has come
We're forgiven and whole
The work of salvation done
Once forever for every soul
We now have the power
The truth and the light
To proclaim to all mankind
And yes my friend I've found
Happiness in Jesus lasts
Through the toils and snares of this life
I've a hope that never dies
I'm alive now and forevermore
Because happiness in Jesus lasts.
Happiness in Jesus lasts.

Do You Know?

Do you know what I mean
     when I say that I love you?
Do you know what I mean
     when I say I care?
Do you know what I mean
     when I say that I miss you?
Do you know what I mean
     when I say I wish you were here?

O My children,
I love you so much more
than you'll ever know
With a love brighter
than the sun in the sky
O how I love you
My blessed little children
How I wish
I could steal you away
from all your business
So I could hold you
and tell you the secrets
of the universe
But even more
I long to hold you and whisper
I'll love you until
the time you know is no more.

O precious children
when will you hear that I love you?
When will you believe
I desire your intimacy?

O how I love you
My blessed children
I want you to know
I mean every word I say
I long for nothing more
than to hold you near
and whisper your name
And tell you
all the secrets of My heart
Just look my way
and I'll give you My hand.

When I say I love you
I mean I am committed
I am always right at your side
With a burning desire
for you to know Me fully
I'm waiting to come inside
to give you all authority
to advance My Kingdom wide.
I'm standing by you
with all power and might
to defeat every foe.
But even more
I just long to hold you
until you know without a doubt
that you are Mine
And I will love you for all time
A time that will never cease
because I never die.

When I say I care
It means I will listen
I'm never too busy to hear
It means you have My attention
and I'm devoted to your every care

I rejoice when you rejoice
and I cry when you mourn
I long to fulfill and share
your every dream and longing
to give you all I own.
But even more,
I just long to hold you
until you know without a doubt
that you are Mine
And I love you
just as you are.
Do you know that you
are My precious one?

Dominion

Arise spirit of man
Quiet your soul's mind
From the well of peace
That never runs dry
Be still and know
Jehovah Jireh cannot lie.

God is my refuge and strength
My shelter, tower and provider of need
He's my redeemer
Might and song
Consuming fire
Broken Bread
Communion Wine.

Spirit guide this body
In which You reside
To the Promised Land
Of prosperity and fine wine
Fill us, O God, Your people
With faith, hope and love
So we walk with You on this earth
As we will someday above.

Alpha and Omega
Beginning and End
Alef and Tov
My Yes and Amen
Penetrate my heart
Search me deep within
Soften my stony heart
Of my sins I repent
Cleanse all that's foul in me
So I can see You again.

Shine light on my blindness
The pride that looks at outward man
While forgetting
That You look within.
In spite of imperfections
You place Your treasure within
We each with the calling
More souls to win

Open my deaf ears Lord
That only appear to care
Because though hearing
My thoughts are not there.
Tune my ears to hear You
To more than words said
To guide and encourage
Those oppressed by spirits and men.

I cry out with my whole heart
Help me O Lord
I long to keep Your statues
And can't do it without You

Hold my tongue
When it starts to speak too soon
Without thinking first
what You would do
Sift my careless words
Incinerate them with Your fire
So I walk in Your desires

Lord I confess my attitude
Too often is not right
I'm more concerned about myself
Than others at my side
Renew a right spirit
Deep within my heart
Wash away my pride
Make me a blessing
More compassionate and kind.

Egypt

Meditations:
Romans 1:28-32
Hebrews 10:23
Galatians 5:1
I Thessalonians 4:7-8; 5:19

In this state of mystical confusion
Could it be my life is just an illusion?
A series of events that flash by
No rhyme, no reason
No answer why??
I look around and I see
Life staring back at me
And yet there is a barrier between
What I know and what I see.
There is a barrier
A force field I can't penetrate
Oh God help me
I'm trapped in a cage!
The key is lost and I fear I must stay
Alone in this forsaken place
That darkens more with each passing day.
How long O Lord must I stay
Alone in this invisible place?
I cry out and no one hears
I scream so loud it should deafen ears.
I wait…
I'm sure there must be a reply
And…
Silence.
…
..
.

In pity…I cry.

Enduring Grace

Against Thee and Thee only
Have I sinned
And done this evil
In Thy sight.
Since my sin is against Thee
Before Thee
I stand in repentance.

From Thee I seek wisdom
And bow in humility
Desiring to be obedient..
Almighty and Most High God
Creator of heavens and earth
I acknowledge my sinful ways;
My pursuit of worldly treasures,
Enlightenment and intellect,
The power to persuade,
And my aspirations to be esteemed by man.

At Your altar, O God, I surrender selfish desires
Stubbornness, rebelliousness, independence, and
hardened heart.
I confess my failure to read Thy Word,
Pray in accord with Your Holy Spirit,
And continually seek Thy way.

I have neglected to listen to Your voice,
Fix my eyes steadfastly upon Your Holy face,
See the needs of my neighbors,
Live a Godly life,
And be an example in the world I live.

I confess to You, Sovereign King,
That my sinful ways are rooted in pride,
Lust, self-preservation, and temptations
From the evil one
Springing forth from carnal seeds
Of immaturity.
In failing to heed Thy Word
I nourished the desires of my flesh;
Serving to strengthen
The insatiable hunger
While my spirit starved
And my bones protruded.

Malnourished, my vulnerability to temptation
increased…
And in my weakness of spirit, I succumbed to sin
As a leper I turned away from the Beloved
And cried "Unclean…unclean!!"
Outcast and alone in the darkness,
Along the path of indifference, self-pity, laughter and
folly,
I turned from those seeking to deliver me
        to heal my diseases and transgressions
            and rejected Your loving grace,
            forgiveness, and protection.

After such ignorance and folly
My soul continued to want.
I had eaten and was not satisfied,
Drank and my thirst not quenched.
I relaxed and enjoyed life in vain
But had not peace within.

In deficiency, I opened Thy Word
Yet was cursed with guilt and condemnation
As the Word blurred before my eyes
I beheld my sin
Saw the evil one's grin
And cried out in sorrow and fear,
"My God what have I done?"

I perceived the severity of my transgression
And bowed humbly in trembling fear
"Against Thee and Thee only have I sinned
and done this evil in Thy sight.."
While yet in my filth and unrighteousness
Thy Word began flowing from my lips.

And I remembered the day when I feasted
At Thy table, an undeserving, yet honored guest.
And in my spirit I felt the tension and striving
From both glory and evil
Quarrelling for my soul.
Then I heard the voice of the Lord say:
"Rest and clear thy mind
Evil desires my Word to condemn you
While you are unable to discern."

Then I heard the demon proclaim:
"Read now of the judgment
in your God's Word."
And shaken, I rested, fully aware of the lies he breathed.

As my mind cleared with morning light
I again sought the throne of the Lord
And bowed humbly at His feet of grace.
With broken and contrite heart
I surrendered to my God

And I heard a voice say:
"Hear now and understand My words
and your journey shall be steadfast on the path
that leads to eternal joy…"

"My Child, there is permissiveness
in the laws of man
such that allow actions and attitudes
contrary to the teaching of My Holy Word.
Little one, you are born of My Spirit
You've already been cleansed through and through
So there are ways of man, though lawful in his sight
That are unholy to Me and unacceptable for you.
I require holiness, ownership, and authority.

Your sin is not an earthy offense
It is one of indifference, foolishness and disobedience,
But one of treason, nonetheless.
Man will not condemn your actions
Though he may call you a hypocrite
For man pursues a wicked way
Led by the father of lies
Who seeks not My face.

I know your weakness as human flesh
That your mind and heart are often willing
Yet the will power of flesh so weak
I know, for I am Creator of all
Even the dust of thee.

But you must understand my precious child,
Hearken forth your ear:
Your choices today shall pave the way
Hence forth from your journey here.
If you seek the way of the ruler of the earth
Or live casually towards me
You live in danger of straying away and rejecting
the grace of the Prince of Peace;
for your each and every action My child
is either towards or away from Me.

Yes, you have erred My child,
But do not turn away in shame
Turn again unto Me now
While your ears know My Name as Yahweh.
Heed the voice of the Lord your God
Let not the tempter persuade you further into his abyss.
Renounce his power and his name where you stand
In the name of Jesus Christ the Lord
And fix your eyes once again and march towards
The Eternal Promised Land.
Do not rely on your own strength
Only I am able to deliver you.
I tell you the truth
It is evil who says that I will punish you
Even if you repent
It is Satan who says you are condemned
And have forfeited your peace forever
That your sins are unforgivable
And you're encaged in your sin
And cannot be delivered.

I, and only I, tell you the truth
For Satan is the father of lies
Who is he to say, whom I will forgive
Was it he that was crucified
Or that rose again?

Do not hearken a moment to his deception
Lest you fall into his guilt and pit of damnation
Where eternal fire awaits those who rejected
The grace of the God Most High.

Hearken your ears unto my words
And turn from your wicked ways
Seek again and again my Holy face
With open heart and mind
That I may once again fill you
With my wisdom and peace
And empower you
With My overcoming strength."

Praise be to He
Lord God Almighty
Who was and is and is to come
Come quickly Lord Jesus, Come.

Ever Mindful

You offered Yourself
As the Son of God
To purchase slaves
And make them
Sons of love

Do we now think
It is asking too much
To honor You?

I'm not my own
But bought with a price
Your blood on the cross
Paying my debt
To pave the way
For us all to move from
The house of slavery
Into the Kingdom of God

Remind me Father
I too often forget
I am not my own
Rather bought with a precious gift
The blood of Jesus Christ.

And all that I have
Is from Your original plan
And is Yours not mine
My purpose and place
Now and forevermore
Is to glorify You.

No more a slave
Now a Son
Teach me to love
As a reflection of You.

Evidence
Meditation: Psalm 95:1-7

The rocks and trees cry out His name
Longing to see Him again
To hear His voice, feel His touch
And see the face of the One they love
Forever faithful 'til He comes.

Mighty branches wave in praise
Of His Majestic Name
Power, Glory, Honor
Wonderful Savior of mankind
Beautiful creation designer
Of heavens high and earth below.

O rocks and trees cry out His name
Shout His highest praise
Shout loudly so no man can ignore.
Awaken the slumbering from his sleep.
Shake the earth to startle the slothful heart.
Open our eyes to creation's song.

Spark in us the love in You
May we feel Your kiss
In the morning dew
We on earth long for Your touch
While demons tremble
At the thought.

O rocks and trees
Teach our hearts to sing
Forever faithful
Day after day
With the obedience
You display.

Evidence Manifest

Meditation: Psalm 95:1

I see Your wonder
In the sunset and its rise
The colors proclaim Your splendor
Across the expanse of skies
I see Your majesty
In the sea billows roll
In mountain peaks exalted
In the stars at night.

Reaching, longing
My soul yearns for You
Seeking with great desire
Only Your Spirit's truth.

I feel Your love so tender and miraculous
When I hold a newborn child
And I know Your tender mercies
In the compassion of loving eyes.

All creation sings Your glory
Morning sun and night starlight,
Author of the seasons
Yet, You're here at my side.

I hear Your power in the thunder's roar
The mighty winds and raging fire
And in all these I know, You are so near
Speaking in so many ways
We so oft fail to hear.

Father, Creator
Wonder of my very soul
Sharpen my senses
Draw me ever close
I long to see and hear You
More than anything

Purge from me distractions
That blind and deafen me.

I know You hear the infant's cry
And see the pain in my hardened heart.
Take my hands; I lift them to You
Raise me up, Master of the Universe.

Draw me nearer, nearer still
Until my spirit joins the song
Just as You, the Holy Ghost
And Jesus are One.

Exaltation
{John 7:18}

"He who speaks from himself
Seeks his own glory
But he who seeks the glory of God
No unrighteousness is in him."

Winds blow
Cross pollinate
Transplant
Harvest rise
Separate and bind
Tares of the soul
True wheat bows
In humility to the reaper
For exaltation
By Your hand.

Eyes of Love

He sees your tears
He feels your hurt and pain,
He knows the paths
You've trodden in shame.
But when His eyes of love
Fall upon your stony heart
The hardness of years of suffering
Melts
In His fiery gaze
And your heart heals
In His embrace
As you behold
His pure eyes of Love.

He sees your broken heart
Confused and failing.
He feels the stab in your back
When men have slandered.
He sees your broken spirit
When it seems you've lost it all.
He hears your cries in the night
When you weep all alone.

O Lord, my God
Unveil our eyes today
To see mankind in the image
Of which he was made.
So as it was in the beginning
When You called Your creation "good"
Shall it ever be
That we Your people
Esteem and behold Your Beloved
As You did on Calvary
When Your love poured out without measure
And covered a multitude of sin
In the garden of grace we call "Born Again."

With Your eyes, I long to see
Each man, woman and child
Only with Your eyes of love
In unity,
Beholding the unveiled face
Joining another in embrace
With the eyes of Love.

FAITH ACRONYMS

Fervent
Adherence
In
True
Harmony

Fact
Already
In
The
Heavenlies

Firm
Assurance
Infilling
The
Heart

Our God of Faith is a:

Firm foundation
Able to
Illuminate
Truth in
Humans

Fascination

I need to bow down
I need to rise up
I need to raise my hands
To honor Your Holy Name.
I need to walk with You
Right alongside You
All of my days.

I need to worship
Sing Your praises
I need to be silent, too
Soak in Your presence
Just be with You
Yes, just be with You
All of my days.

Father

Father above
I hear Your voice.
I hear You
Rustling in the trees.
O Mighty God
It's You, I long to please.
Yes it's You I long to please.
It's only You I need.
My mighty refuge
My redeeming King
Strength of my heart
Forever and ever
Make me more
Like Thee.

O Mighty God
My Savior and Lord
I will shout Your majestic Name
Until the silence sings
Until the silence sings.
O Mighty One
Yeshua, Adonai
We Your children sing Your praise
Forever.
Forever and ever
Forever and ever
Forever and ever
We will dance and sing Your praise.

For You are Holy
You are Holy
You are Holy
Around Your throne we sing.
Forever and ever
Forever and ever
Forever and ever
Your Name we raise!

Father, We Love You

Father, we love You
You are the Lord
We lift our hands
To You adore
We sing of Your Holy Name
We lift our eyes to Heaven
And raise our hands to praise
To praise You
To praise You
O Lord we love
To praise You.

Fault Line

Please don't find faults with me
I know well what they are
I've lived with myself
Since the day I was born
I know what I do well
And where I fall short
So please don't find fault with me
Just for the sport.

I know it's easier to pass judgment
Than to rehabilitate the criminal
But when I long to change the way I am
Judgment condemns to hopelessness
All the potential longing to spring forth from my well.

Please just love me as I am
Warts, corns, and scars
It's the only chance I have to germinate
And yield a harvest for the Lord.

I know I'm not always lovable
And sometimes push you away
I know I say things without speaking
And mouth things I ought not say.

I know I lack discipline
And many other skills
I could go on and on
But no purpose would it fulfill.

Just let it be said
I know I'm not always pleasant
Or what you would hope me to be
But I hope you can find it in you
To look deeply for the good in me.

It seems to me when bad spews forth
It destroys all my worth
And I need hope to go on
Because if the good does not take root
My life will end before I'm born.

So if you can
Treat me delicately
'Til my tender shoots grow strong
I will never forget you
When Harvest Time is come.

Fixation

Fix my eyes on You Lord
Steady my gaze
Focus my attention
So I do not stray.

Let the splendor of Your glory
Enthrall my soul
Let Your beauty hold me
Until I am whole
In You.

I cling to You
Creator
Savior
Lover of my soul.
I live
I breathe
I live forevermore
In You.

Follow Me
Galatians 6:7-10

Follow Me, follow Me
I don't want you my friend bound in the chains
        of trying to please man.
Man is not capable of My perfect acceptance
        because of his flesh.
Just as the Covenant of Old allowed for covering sins
        only for a time
        until perfect remission had come
        so it is with you;
this time now being the time of preparation.

I have allowed events in your life to teach you
        to bring you to Myself.
Even when it seemed all was against you,
        I held you in the palm of My hand.
You are right to have sought My face
        continue therein.
Continue seeking Me and My ways
        and you will find the favor
        and acceptance your heart desires.
I AM the Lord your Creator
I know the intimate needs of your heart
        and I knew them before your knitting
        in your mother's womb.
I formed you knowing My desires for you
Trust my way and seek only Me.
My Word is true
        It says if you seek Me – you will find Me
        And find Me you WILL.
        It is My promise to you.
Hence I say, keep your eyes toward Me.
In Me, you will find blessings
        beyond your imagination.

In Me waits a Promised Land
truly a land of milk and honey
        for your soul
        prepared only for My children.
It is eternal food for the total restoration
        of your spirit and soul.
This promise holds true for the days to come
        when My people shall join Me forevermore
        but for those who believe and seek my face
        in the earthly life, it is also true.
I am your God and it is I that has spoken
I speak only truth
The truth that sets men free
But hear Me, My child, you must believe.
Hear again, the truth shall set you free;
For what the Son sets free is free indeed.
Fear not My child
It is My light shining before you.
It is the light of My glory,
Follow Me.

For Jesu

There's a life beyond this world of troubles
A safe harbor just beyond the sea billow's roll
A peace more still than a baby sleeping
A beauty more pure than fresh driven snow.

There's a freshness exceeding
          the Spring rains' cleansing,
A taste more quenching
          than the mountain spring's supply,
A voice more soothing
          than soft bagpipes singing,
And a knowing deeper in the soul
          than intellectual heights.

These weave through our lives
Yet our soul is not satisfied
Until in our emptiness we are made whole.
And it's then that life's real meaning
Becomes embedded in loving others so deeply
we see and know them as our own;
when loving more than our measure
penetrates our entire soul!

For it's not until then
that we hear our brother's hungry cry.
It's not until then
that we see beyond his skin
and see our naked self inside
and feel his lonely shivering at night.
No, it's not until we are emptied
of the passion of our lives,
and it's not until we are blinded,
that we gain our sight!

Lord strike me blind, deaf and mute,
Remove my hands and my eyes,
If with the senses with which You've blessed me
I fail to see You in my brothers' eyes!!

So I write this for Jesu
And all of them in this world
That we do and do not yet know.
I'll sing this song for all the Jesus'
Until mankind's greatest challenge is overcome;
Be it tomorrow,
Or be it in Heaven,
May God fill us with His Holy love.

So my prayer is that we'll find
A love that's yours and mine.
A love for all time,
Now and forever,
One moment at a time.

Foreshadowing

Abraham was climbing up the mountain with Isaac
When he heard his son say:
"Father, where's the sacrifice?"
Abraham answered: "God will provide."
But I have to wonder if in his mind
Abraham was crying, Lord, O Lord, why?
O Lord, where is the ram?
O Lord, where is the ram?
When a voice announced:
"Turn around my friend."

Noah and his sons were told to build an ark
That water would flood the earth
Where sin had left its mark
Don't you wonder if in his mind
Noah was crying,
Lord, O Lord, why?
O Lord when will the rain end?
O Lord when will the rain end?
When a voice spoke:
"Forty days and forty nights."

Then there was David
A boy tending sheep
Confident he would not suffer loss
Against his challenger.
Listen with me,
Can you hear him say,
"Where's this giant Goliath
The one I will slay
And why is Israel's army so afraid?"
O Lord, I put my trust in You
O Lord, You are faithful and true
Young David soon to be King
And a man after God's own heart.

See Daniel thrown in the lion's den
With no charge against him
Other than praying to the only God
All others forsaking.

O Lord I see the lions
Their snarling teeth do shine
But they are no match for the angels
Who their mouths do bind
O Lord, praise be to Your Name
Lord, O Lord, Your glory I proclaim
O Lord, praise be to Your Name
Lord, O Lord, Your glory I proclaim
O Daniel,
By faith you were saved!

Jesus' disciples traveled with Him by road
Ate and drank with Him
As parables, He told
He chose the weak and created the bold.
Can't you hear them now
The afternoon He died?
Hanging between two thieves
Bloody and crucified:
"O Lord, where is our King?
Lord, O Lord, where is our King?
As the Father answers:

"O My children, you will soon see
After three days in the grave
It was for your freedom
Your King's hanging on that tree
Death swallowed up in Victory."

Forever

{Deuteronomy 23:47; Psalm 118:1,24,27,29; Revelation 5:1,9}

Boldly come to the Throne;
Children enter in.
Today is the day
Rejoice and be glad.
God Almighty is the Lord
He showers us
With the light of His Word.
Children rise and come forth
Giving thanks for His mercy.
He is great and to be adored;
His love endures forevermore

We rejoice for the curse is removed
We are redeemed
By the blood of the Lamb
Our names are written
In the Book of Life
His blessings
Indeed for tomorrow
But even more, for today
Hear my praise to You Lord
To You I rejoice
And to You I sing.

Forever – all my yesterdays
Forever – yes, even today
Forever – every tomorrow
In His eyes, forgiven the same

In His eyes – forever
In His hands – forever
In His mercy – forever
In His glory – forever
Forever, yes forever
Forever, here I'll stay!

Freedom

Loosen my feet from this ground
Break the tethers that have me bound
Destroy the restraints holding me down
A Deliverer, I have found.
In Him, unconditional love abounds.
I know His voice
And His warring shofar's sound
As I see the nails pound
I hear the cry of "VICTORY!!"
And the angels' voices resound with singing
As the heavens and earth shout "Freedom!"

Genesis to Revelation

In the beginning God created
The heavens and the earth
And formed man in His image
Right from the dirt

He wouldn't let them be denied
No they weren't to be denied
Until the Messiah came
He wouldn't let them be denied

In days of Old, God lived with man
In the Ark of the Covenant
And forgiveness came from sacrifices
On the Day of Atonement

So they would not be denied
So they would not be denied
For until the Messiah came
He wouldn't let them be denied

Holy, Holy, Holy
Is the Lord God Almighty
Who was and is and is to come
Hallelujah and Amen

And when in the Garden
Satan deceived Eve
God knew of the day to come
When Jesus would set men free

Then one day there was a cry
From John in the wilderness
Make straight your paths
For the Kingdom is at hand

Jesus was born to us a babe
In Bethlehem
Fully God and fully man
He died for our sins

So we are not denied
We are not denied
The Savior came and shed His blood
So we are not denied

Three days in the grave
They thought Him dead and gone
But glory be He rose again
And ascended to the Throne

And we are not denied
No, we are not denied
Jesus defeated death
And we are not denied

And to fulfill man's greatest need
He sent the Comforter
Who seals us with the Lamb of God
And brings joy to our heart

And we are not denied
And we are not denied
The Comforter comes with His life
And we are not denied

Because of God's grace and love
For my unworthy soul
Forever I will praise His Name
For making me whole.

And I am not denied
Now I am not denied
Though scarlet were my sins
Now the righteous, I am called.

Glory Be to the Lamb

Holy, Holy, Holy
Glory be to the Lamb
Holy, Holy, Holy
To the Great I AM
To You be the highest praise
As we exalt Your Name
For no greater love is there
Than by Your Son slain.

Holy, Holy, Holy
Glory be to the Lamb
Holy, Holy, Holy
Saved by His Word
His Name, His blood
I exalt Your Name forever
And bow obediently
I receive and give Your blessings freely
Teach me more to believe
And glory be to the Lamb.

God Said

God said, "Hey little boy
with the curly dark hair;
Do you know what I called you for?
You'll be the Savior of mankind?"

"There's more I'll tell you soon
But for now learn of Me
Give Me time and know who I AM
I AM, Your Father
And I'll stand by you."

"Hey young man it's time
To enact Our plan for all mankind.
Go to John at the River;
Go and be baptized
To fulfill all righteousness.
There's more I'll tell You soon
But for now
The Spirit's waiting at the Jordan."

Jesus heard the Lord
And hiked to the Jordan
John peered at Him and said,
"I should be baptized by You."
And Jesus replied with fire in His eyes
"Let it be so for now."

Out of the water, John saw Him rise
He saw the dove and heard the
voice above
"This is my Beloved Son
In Whom I am well pleased."

Out in the desert the tempter waited
To bring down He who would hold
The keys to his destiny
Only to find with each trap he baited
Jesus answered thrice,
"It is written…it is written…
It is written."

Tempted in all ways as we
Jesus stood against the lies and power
Of our enemy
Not for His own fame
But to please the Father
From whence He came.

He taught His disciples
The Kingdom of God
He healed the sick
And loved His enemies
Forgave sin and paid the price
Unrighteous men could never pay.

Lead me out of this world
Out of myself where I have lived
I want to be with You
I lift my hand to You for help
I'm so ready to get out
Of the chains that hold me down.

Teach me Lord, how to pray
And show me Jesus like John that day
Not the traditions and ways of men
But the way that leads
To holiness.
Again I hear You say:
"It is finished."
Please show me Lord what that means
In the actions of my day
Put it deep within my heart
As a new song to sing.

The Kingdom of God is near
Come in without fear
Tell everyone who'll hear
The blood of Jesus sets you free
It's time to praise
To dance and sing.

Gonna Align My Feet

Traveling through the valley
I see the mountain ahead
I know along the journey
Will be dangers of death
But I'm gonna climb that mountain
By following my guide
The Light of day
And North Star at night

Gonna align my feet
In step with the Lord's
He is the leader
I love and adore
In the miles we travel
I'll never be alone
He'll be there with me
On that untrodden road

I'm gonna run those spiritual waters
Maneuvering with firm grip
Safety gear with me
If my boat should tip
Just like that mountain above
With avalanches and slides
I see the whirlpools
And the high falls
But none shall overtake me
With the Lord as my guide.

Good, Good God

You are a good, good God
You're a good, good God
What can I say
What can I do
For a good, good God like You?

You are a good, good God
Such a good, good God
You bring sun and rain
On the righteous and unjust, too
You love the redeemed
And those who reject You
You are light in darkness
Hope in distress
You are the answer we are seeking
In the midst of our mess

You are seed to the sower
And the beam of the evening star
Miracle working power
Even when we don't believe
Master of Creation
Even when we can't see

Father to the fatherless
Rain to drought-stricken lands
Living water to the thirsty
Heartbeat to the dead
Love, power and passion
For all mankind

You are a good, good God
You're a good, good God
What can I say
What can I do
For such a good, good
God like You.

Graffiti and Stone Hinges

Meditations: James 1:5-8
                   Revelation 2:4-5

I've tracked the circle round and round
Elated in highs and drowned in downs
Now back to the great crevasse
Full speed ahead – life flying past
Will I stop at the edge or sail on past?
One foot on the brake, the other on the gas
Spinning, rolling – out of control
Gaining momentum
Over the edge I go
The beauty around now only a blur
All that was, I left behind.

I grasped for control
Until it bent my mind and broke my neck
Like layers of ice on a weak tree branch
It once made sense…that life behind
But now in confusion
Life only an illusion
Another small remnant
I leave behind
From another day…another time…
The writing on the wall is mine.

For Sale: Esau's Birthright – Cheap
Sold: Birthright for Soup

What will temporal hungers tempt us to sell?
Our inheritance in Heaven for the fires of Hell?

Grief

The blackness surrounds
And engulfs my soul
Those black and green clouds
From which whirlwinds blow.
The emptiness cries
Like fear in a storm,
While I grasp for stability
From fraying cord;
As I wonder if I'm insane
Or this is just the norm.

Where do I go
And what do I do
With such emptiness and pain?
And what could anyone else do
If they cared anyway?
Am I bound to this demon
For the rest of my days?
Or is this a fleeting haze?
Jesus do you understand
This grief of my soul?

He Sent Forth the Word

I wish I could tell you
that I've never doubted
        never been discouraged or deceived.
Yet, it has happened, but I'm thankful
        and praise my God for teaching me
how to defeat the enemy.

He sent forth the Word of forgiveness and salvation.
There is no other way to the Father, except by Him.
He sent forth the Word for healing and restoration.
He sent it forth so we could live
        in the favor of His peace.
And all I'm asking now is – will you receive?

After wandering years in the desert,
I'd had enough of my sin and needed something more;
So I received His offer of salvation,
healing and restoration
for my thirsty soul.
It was so simple
He sent forth His Word and it was so.

Now I rest in blessed peace
shalom, total fullness.
I am complete, nothing broken
for I'm totally whole.
No more wandering,
I have committed my life, my goals,
my every breath --- to the work of God.

I know His Word is true
I read it over and o'er
and I have learned not to live by bread alone.
My faith has made me whole
just like He taught in books of Old and New.
Now I'm girded with armor
and I drink from the river
that satisfies my soul.

He Still Cries

Jesus cried
"It is finished"
And died on that tree.
Died for our redemption,
You and me.
And the Father still
Cries for souls
To visit His Holy place,
Where the veil
No longer separates.

People of God
Can you hear?
Can you hear His cry
To seek His Holy face?
To lay down our lives?
For His embrace
And life with Him?
How is it we can walk away
When we could have everything
If with Him we'd stay?

Can you hear that He still cries?

<u>Healing Touch</u>

Jesus, I love You
      You have done so much.
You brought me a true love
      and that healing touch.
How can I show You
      my love in return?
And when I asked to hear Your voice,
      This is what I heard:

"Cease from your labors
just come and receive -
Not crumbs under the table
but life abundantly.
You are the reason
I came to live and die.
The love I have for you
Is the fire burning in my eyes."

Heart Song

Quiet my heart - Quiet my soul
I can't hear You in all this noise

Steal me away
From everything
That leads me astray
Or keeps me from You…

You are the heartbeat
Of my innermost being
Pumping life
Head
to
toe
You are the very
Breath I breathe
Infusing life
Into my soul

Water to the thirsty
Food to the starved
Freedom for the captive
Broken chains for the bound
Rain to the drought-stricken
And to forests burning
A turning wind
Of life to the dead

Sound to the deaf
Sight to the blind
Friend to the lonely
A home for the wandering
Rest for the weary
Peace to the mind
Light in darkness
Love without end…

Heartbeat of God

I am a tempo
A drum beating cadence
Reverberating on and on
The heartbeat of my Father
The One who loves the world.

Love beating heavily
Flowing from Heaven steadily
The blood of Jesus
The dance of reconciliation
Relationship unfailing
The estranged, now sons and daughters
United again with Him as before the Fall.

Come and join the tempo
March on the pavement
And on demons who've overtaken
That which God gave us.
For love beats steadily
Flows from Heaven with authority
The blood of Jesus
Purity and power
Restoring us securely
Under His wings.

And He shall rule forever
Because the blood river cleanses all sin.
And He shall rule forever
His priests and kings reigning
And twenty-four Elders
Casting crowns
Before His throne

I am a tempo
The heartbeat of God.

<u>Higher</u>

Jesus, You came to
fulfill Your covenant
to pay the price
to bring us back to You
Now the veil is
torn from the top down
granting us access
to the Holy of Holies

So we can come closer
We can come closer
The veil is torn wide from top down
So we can go higher
So we can go higher
So we can go higher
I can feel my heart pound
with love for You.

There is no greater love
Than His for us
Sacrifice to redeem us
Fellowship restored

All so you and I
Can come closer
Can come closer
The veil is torn wide from top down
So I can go higher
Come with me and go higher
To the foot of His throne
To the foot of His throne.

His Wisdom

Meditations:
Isaiah 12:2; Proverbs 9:10

Satan's lies don't change God's truth
Sugar coating only conceals rotten fruit
I will not throw my pearls before swine
God will reap a harvest in His time.

Satan's laugh must loudly screech
When God is blamed for evil deeds.
Is there a greater lie than a human
Becoming a god by his own strife?

It is His wisdom I seek
Men are frail, weary and weak.
Almighty One, protect the harvest
For which I was sown
For that special purpose only You know.
Guide Your child in wisdom
God of Heaven
Creator of my Soul!

Hold to My Teaching

Meditations:
John 8:31-32, 36; Luke 4:18-19; James 1:25

If you hold to My teaching
Then you are My disciple
You will know the truth
And it will set you free
My cross shattered the yoke
That burdened and bound you
Stand fast with Me
And live in perfect liberty.

In my youth, I walked away
Temptation and appeals
Drew me from the God I loved,
But then the way that seemed so right
Turned a dark and weary gray
In shame I cried
And returned to My Father's arms.

Then He said to me:
If you hold to My teaching
Then you are My disciple
You will know the truth
And it will set you free
My cross shattered the yoke
That burdened and bound you
Stand fast with Me
And live in perfect liberty.

Now I praise God
No longer am I ashamed
He brought me life and true joy
Delivering me from that wretched day
I will rejoice always
For the precious Lamb of God.

Holy, Holy, Holy

Holy, Holy, Holy
Lord God, You are mighty
As angels bow down
And praise Your Splendor
One day the Earth will
Sing of Your Glory
With Holy, Holy, Holy
Unending songs resound.

Holy, Holy, Holy
You are the Holy One
There is no other One
Among gods or man.
Your power and love
A triune testimony
Holy, Holy, Holy
Redeemer of my soul.

Holy, Holy, Holy
There is no other worthy
Spotless Lamb of God
Who took away the sins of the world
Beloved brother, teacher and rabbi
Friend of the outcast
Holy, Holy, Holy
Son of Man and God Alive.

Holy, Holy, Holy
Thy Kingdom come
Thy will on earth be done
Man and beast proclaim Thy praise
Submitting to Thy Holy reign
Hand in hand with peace's banner raised
Holy, Holy, Holy
To Him who was, and is and is to come!

Home – Ode Of The Prodigal

I hungered and thirsted
For the treasures of the world
Only to suffer from failure to thrive
So I sought the most noble and highest morals
In religious men
And my stomach gnawed at my backbone again.

I cried, fasted, and rent my clothes
Smeared ashes on my face and mourned
But no god or man came alongside
Or wiped the relentless tears I cried.

So I ran swiftly after the wind
Finding nothing on the road to nowhere and then
I searched the heavens and earth deep within
To uncover more questions with no answers.

I ran again
Like the Jonah from God
To my own demise
Emerging like he
On the beach with a stench.

So I abandoned all I couldn't see
Couldn't feel or understand
And tossed You away
Like junk mail and old magazines
To walk the road of the prodigal son
Believing I was an illegitimate one.

I wrestled with bitterness as an orphan
In the sea of sons and daughters.
I denied there being a rift in my soul
Accusing the accusers of mental infirmity.

For years I stared down the barrel of emptiness
With no redeeming light
I sought wisdom and worth
From crumbling dry wells.

I bathed in geysers of sulfur
In the limestone mountains and pits
Homeless with nowhere to go
I walked naked in winter enduring frostbite
Til I felt no pain
Only to survive for the summer to end.

All my life I never knew the name of my God
Till I heard a child cry Daddy
And arms from high reached down low.
Quickly my running ceased
My blind eyes opened, my deaf ears heard
As I fell on my skinned and scarred knees.

Suddenly, oh so suddenly
I knew my rightful place
I understood I was an heir
As I ate my first satisfying meal
At the cross of amazing grace.

With my eternal Father God
I now know my place
An heir, a child of destiny
I no longer live by bread alone
And I hunger and thirst no more
Since my God brought me home.

<u>Hope</u>

I tried to tell what I saw as truth
And the story I told was not understood
And I left that place isolated in my soul
Isolated and all alone
Isolated
No one to comfort my soul.

Too scared to share anymore
I stuffed it all inside and I swore
No one would ever see me vulnerable again
Yet the soul hurts
When you're isolated
Alone and empty
No comfort for the soul...
A man's spirit dies when it's left
All alone

I hear the music on stage
Men and women gathered to pray
Laughing in the hallway
And no one knows
I'm grieving all alone
Behind a locked door
With no lights on
Cause there's no worldly comfort
I dare to know
It'll have to be God
Cause there's no human comfort
For this soul
Misunderstood and isolated
All alone

Life will go on here
While no one knows
The creative miracle
God's working in my soul
As He wraps me in love
Surrounding me like a butterfly's cocoon
And after a season
The new will emerge
And fly away
With a new purpose
No more bondage
No more fear
No longer alone.

But until that day
I'll wait here for God to come
And hold me in His arms of love
No more pain
No longer alone
While He comforts
My frail soul.

In this silence
My flesh cries out
But my spirit sings…
To my weak flesh.
He grants strength
To open the door of my heart
And try to love once more.
No more darkness
No longer alone
The enemy's lost
I am loved
And no longer alone

Thank you Lord
For comforting my soul
And for a love greater
Than I've ever known.

Hope in Christ

Mediation: I Corinthians 15:19

The Lord Your God is with you
His power gives you victory
The Lord delights in you
And gives you new life
He blesses with favor
All those who love Him
Be thankful and base your happiness
On your hope in Christ.

If God be for you
Who can stand against you?
Give no regard
To situations in this life.
Know that all is well
In the hands of the Master,
That your God in Heaven
Hears every cry.

Oh my soul, praise the Lord
I'm healed of my afflictions
But even more
I'm forgiven
My life is redeemed
No longer do I cling
To anyone or thing
But the Rock of Ages.

I Am

I am Your God
I want to be remembered
Glory thunders as I make myself known
I give you dreams and visions
I AM the King of Glory
The declarer of new things
Creator of the beginning
I AM the answer to your deepest desires
I AM the cloud of Old
The Bright and Morning Star
The Comforter
The firm but gentle hand
I AM goodness and kindness to every man

I AM the Ark of the Covenant
Communing with you
The breech between heaven and earth
I tempt no one
For I know no evil
But test your heart against the deceitfulness
Of the evil one
I stretch forth My hand to you
For I AM your righteousness
I came to you in Jesus
So you could know Me face to face
I died on the cross
Your sins to wash away
To restore you to Myself

I AM the refiner
Of your clay
Your healer, too
The giver of life's abundance
I have great plans for each of you

I want you to believe in Me
Fear Me with reverence and live
I bring the highest order
More than you can conceive or give
I want to be remembered
If you only knew
How much it is that I love you
You would run to Me
And reign and with authority
At My right hand

You've misunderstood
So much about Me
I want you to know
My purity and truth
I long to make you Holy
So in My presence you can stand
O I long for you to be My child forever
And reign with Me at my right hand.

I Cry Out

I cry out to You, Holy Flame
I cry out to You, Holy God
I cry out to You!
Descend Holy flame
Jesus' blood my salvation
You my righteousness
I've no strength of my own
When I am weak, You are strong
My soul cries for Your fire!

I cry out to You
Come purify
Purify
Purify
Holy Flame
Purge ungodliness
Purify
Purify
I cry out to You!

I cry out to You, Holy Flame
I cry out to You, Holy God
I cry out to You!
Descend Holy Flame
Burn all impurities away
Until I flow in unity with You
No more of my will
There is only You

I bow down in worship
I bow down in worship
I bow down in worship
I lay on Your altar
I burn as worship to You.

I Hear the Father Speaking

I hear the Father speaking
A whisper I perceive
brought by gentle breezes
from the west to the east.
Silently passing,
unheard if not sought -
I hear the Father speaking my name
as though aloud.

I hear the Father speaking
A shout rings in my ears
as thunder crashes
and lightning streaks near.
Raging as a storm
I hear Him pass by.
I know that voice of His
by day and night.

I hear the Father speaking
Peace on earth I hear
as I watch children sleeping
while a choir sings near.
Standing on the promises
Christ the Lord is here,
Blessed be the Name
Jesus calms every fear.

I hear the Father speaking
Though bombs fall my way.
The wars seem never ending -
hate prevails on earth today.

Yet, in this battle
He comforts me still
In the battle I hear His cry
Stand fast!
Victory draws near!

I hear the Father speaking;
Silence draws nigh,
As the flowers bloom in the morning
And the moon serenely shines
Ever so silently
Though imperfect
I'm the delight of His eye
And my spirit calms
With His gentle sigh.

I hear the Father speaking
Though flowers fade after dusk
Rest now He says.
As the moon reveals the frost
I wait patiently -
this winter will pass
And spring waits
A promise so vast.

I hear the Father speaking...
Listen as He says,
"My words spoke creation
and are alive in your hands
How can you not know Me?
How can you not see or hear
When the beauty I've created
Sings in your ear?"

Can you hear Him speaking
It takes faith without a doubt
To perceive His whisper
Or to endure His shout.
To let Him be your comfort
When fear descends as a fog
Yet, if you let Him
His peace will surround.

Do you hear the Father speaking
Near or from afar?
Have you heard of the promise
that He sent His Son for?
Have you drank from the river
that never runs dry?
Have you asked the Savior
for forgiveness and new life?

I hear the Father speaking
"Well done, My faithful one.
Come now to Me
your work on earth is done.
Enter in and see the Book;
your name written there.
Come and see the table
with the feast I've prepared."

I Know the Lies

I know the lies the demons tell
They're etched in my mind and soul
The pictures painted in my memory
Only to God and I known.

I know the lies the demons tell
How wrong can seem so right…
That feelings can be the judge
Which makes us our own god.

I know the lies the demons tell
That forever we'll be bound.
That there is no loving God in Heaven
And no evil one in Hell.

I know the lies the demons tell
That only a vicious God sends souls to Hell.
That evil is proof God doesn't exist
That there's no life after this.

I know the lies the demons tell
From captivity in my sin.
But I prayed for God my spirit and soul to cleanse
So I would never believe those lies again.

I know the lies the demons tell
And knowing I'm no match,
I daily ask for God's discernment
Lest I believe and turn my back.

No more lies will I believe
For my Master delivered me.
He's taken my deceived mind
And given me the mind of Christ.

I Rest High

(Music: Go Rest High on that Mountain -Vince Gill)
(Meditations: John 17:4; Luke 22:31-32)

There are days when my heart is troubled
When lacking faith, I doubt and cry
And Jesus, right now I need You
To reach inside and caress my heart.

Chorus:
I rest high on Your mountain
Father Your will, on earth be done.
Pour Your glory from the Heavens
As we shout love for Your Son.

I confess to You, my Father,
I too often worry and dwell
On those things You say not to
Those things that tear down.

In faith right now, I raise my hands
To receive only the peace You can give.
Father, no more of what I once was
For I now yield to Your will.

My life and all my hopes
I plant them all in You
Given time they'll be a harvest
More bountiful than ten thousand fields.

I Want to Know You

Lord I want to know You
well enough to bare
my heart and soul;
To trust You all of my days
To learn more of Your mercy and grace.
Dare I ask to see Your face
so I can know You
in Your dwelling place?

Lord I want to touch You
so I can know I'm safe.
I want to tell You
my deepest secrets, too
So You can heal
the shame I feel.
I will dare to ask Your forgiveness
because I've heard You care.
Can it really be true, I need to know
that You hear me up there.

Lord I want to know You.
I need Your healing
deep within my heart and soul.
I've tried all I know to do
but my wounds are still there.
Recently I've been told
Your healing grace is still here.
So I'm stepping out in faith
to ask and believe
for You to draw near.

Lord I wait for You in silence
Your voice, I long to hear..
Your words of Truth, love and mercy.
None other satisfies the longing of my soul.
I'll stay with You forever
In You, I've been made whole.

Identity

O God, my Father
Creator of time
Holy Spirit
Comforter of the Vine
Jesus, Savior, Bridegroom
With You I long to dine.

I am Your branch
Grafted into Your vine
Your sap is my strength
My food divine
Redeemer, Re-newer
Of my mind
None ever sweeter
Nor so kind.
Creator, Savior
Love of mine
None ever sweeter
Nor so kind
Pure love and beauty
In me abide
None ever sweeter
Nor so kind
Triune Holy God
I am Thine.

If I Knew That I Knew

If I knew that I knew I pleased my Master, I could rest, find peace and also be energized in the certainty of fulfilling the tasks for which He created me. If my faith would allow my eyes to see and love myself as He loves me, I believe the voices of inadequacy and fear would cease.

What causes this failing of hope in my soul? Do the roots lie in the selfishness and lack of love man shows God and his neighbor? Like the Hebrews of Old is my prevailing sin the desire to return to the slavery of Egypt where at least life was predictable? So quickly God delivered me from Egypt and as they, too long it has taken to rid me of the Egypt mentality within.

Why is my soul weary? Why do I seek to quit so soon? Why do I fail so oft at running the race set before me that Paul speaks of? Will I allow human frailty or sins of the flesh to discourage me from seeking and trusting in the face of my God? Will I be distracted by simple carnal pleasures, the praises of man, intellectual idols, or man's insufficiency as shown by unkindness, lack of love and compassion, or rejection? Will I seek the intellectual or praises of man with such fervor that I heap them up as gold and worship them as idols?

O that I would allow my God to fan His coals ablaze in this body I call flesh, in full consuming confidence and boldness that I AM HIS and no one and no thing is capable of plucking me from the palm of His hand. O that I would soar on currents of air above or the waters below; at peace even in the turbulent storms, unpredictable wind shears, whirlpools and undertows, because I know without doubt or fear that You, my God, are God of all gods and my beloved Master.

And in this eating of the tree of life, I find my true identity. I was created for...Your glory and Your good pleasure - not my own!!! I was created for intimate communion with You, my God!! May that fire burn within me and invade my most carnal appetites, incinerating them as living sacrifices for my King. I long that my love for You O God, be unfeigned and without folly. Understanding in fuller revelation until I meet You face to face, that no man is a mere mortal, but an eternal spirit progressing toward one of two eternal homelands. That the lowliest of all mankind is but a precious creation of Yours, made in Your image. O but that mortal man could grasp the Christ You sent to dwell in us to fulfill the summary of the Law - to first love God with all his heart, soul, strength, and mind and secondly to love his neighbor as himself.

Indeed I need not work so feverishly to please You O God. You, Yourself the work hast done!! My calling is to love and worship You and regard Your creation with the same love You have shown me. Freely I have received, freely I shall give! In this task, O Merciful and Gracious Father, set me ablaze as a raging forest fire or tiny celestial star, whatever Your will for me. It is enough that You loved me enough to not only send a Savior, but Your indwelling, comforting, and guiding Holy Spirit. Wherever I go - empower me by this illumination within, to proclaim Your power and glory alone. For without You, I am nothing; and with You, no man on earth or devil in Hell can quench my calling. I am a child and friend of God forever! Amen and Amen!

Impending Doom

Impending doom overshadows the soul
Like deadly fog in the valley below
Like the blinding haze of raging fire
Obscuring danger lurking 'round.

In darkness and confusion
Danger engulfing every stride
I attempt to make passage
As a navigator amiss.

Slowing rapid pace
Confusion deceitfully swirling
giving birth to lies
Fear and panic swells
Transcending other emotions.

What is truth?
I cannot tell.
How can such an illusion
Appear so real?

In agony, the weary soul seeks refuge
And is turned away
Heart sinking heavily
Blood and tears stain
Where is one to go
To find comfort for a weary soul?

Then above the roar and blinding haze
A soft voice within whispers my name
That transforms despair with love.
Who are you?

In Just a While

Meditation: Haggai 2:6-9
(Rapid tempo)

In just a while
I will shake the heavens
I will shake the earth and sea
Dry lands will tremble
As well as nations.
And all who have decided
Shall come to Me.

And in those days
I will fill this house with Glory
Silver's mine
As is the gold.
And the glory of
The new heaven and earth
Shall be greater
Than that of old.

In the Garden

Meditation: Matthew 26:36-43

It was late in the night
When in the garden, Jesus prayed
All alone while His disciples slept.
He asked them to wake and keep watch
But weary and tired
They closed their eyes instead.

Jesus, I'd like to think
I'd have remained awake
And prayed with You that early morn,
But I've no reason to believe
I'd be any stronger than they
Who traveled at Your side.

Yet in my heart
I wish I could have seen You pray,
"Father if there be any other way
May this cup pass from me
But not my will but thine be done
Keep them safe and unite them as one."

Lord, I confess
I do not understand
What Your ways seem to be always,
But none the less
I know I'm blessed
Because You've forgiven me.

I know today
You sit at the right hand
Of the Father Almighty
Interceding on my behalf
Working miracles today as You did then
Freeing those bound in the chains we call sin.

Jesus I often think of You
Praying in Gethsemane all alone
Broken and knowing the pain You'd endure
When for my sins You'd be crucified
Just to set me free
And yet, just for me, You died.

So when I'm discouraged now
I close my eyes and pray Your prayer;
Father if there be any other way
May this cup pass from me
But not my will but thine be done,
Keep us safe and unite us all as one.

In Your Name

There must be more than this
O breath of God
Breathe deep within
Spirit of God I wait for You
Oh let Your glory fall
Spirit of God fall in this place
Lord have Your way in me
I wait here on bended knee
Tears streak my face
Consuming fire fan into flame
A greater passion for Your Name.

There is mercy for sin
There is safety within
In Your Holy Name
When there's nowhere else to go.

In Your Name
There is strength to remain
To endure beyond all pain and shame
All answers rest in Your Name.

Consuming fire fan into flame
That greater passion for Your Name
In You I'm not cast away
I'm received and loved
Even before I'm changed
Breathe Your life into this soul
Set me ablaze with confidence bold
Consuming fire refine
Til there's no division between

What's Yours and mine.

Indwelling Habitation

Lord, convict and inhabit my spirit and soul
so the depth of Your love impregnates my barrenness
with the living waters of everlasting life
to the extent that I with increasingly greater measure
manifest the essential intimate presence and expectancy
of the love, hope, and power of You, Almighty God,
as a witness of Your perfection, now and forever.
Amen and Amen!!

Intercession

Father, I ask that You grant Your Church the power of intercession that Moses spoke of on behalf of the Israelites in the desert that stayed Your hand against them when he said: "Remember Abraham, Isaac, and Jacob, Thy servants, to whom Thou swearest by Thine ownself, and said to them, 'I will multiply your seed as the stars of heaven, and all this land that I have spoken of will I give unto your seed and they shall inherit it forever.'" Father, I thank you that those of us Gentiles that have been engrafted into Your vine are yet today receivers and inheritors of Your Holy promises.

Father, as Your Child of Promise, by the blood of Christ, I ask You to raise up the righteous among us, as well as, prophets, apostles, teachers, evangelists, and pastors for the perfecting and full equipping of the saints, Your consecrated people. I ask O Father, that the Church heed Your Holy Word and do the work of ministering toward the building up of Your Body; that Your Church might continually develop until we all attain oneness in the faith and the comprehension of the full and accurate knowledge of the Son of God, that we fully mature into the completeness of personality in You, which is nothing less than Christ's own perfection, the measure of the stature of the fullness of Christ and the completeness found in Him. So then, we may no longer like children, be tossed like ships to and fro between variations of teaching and wavering with every changing wind of doctrine, which make men prey of the cunning and cleverness of unscrupulous men, engaged in every shifting form of trickery in inventing errors to mislead whether intentional, from arrogance, or ignorance.

Righteous Holy Father, deliver us from those that have hearts that beat in unison with the heart of the Pharisees, Scribes, and teachers of the Law of Moses as in days of Old – serving You outwardly, but inwardly harboring a hardened, deadened, unhearing and unchangeable heart of stone, suitable only to mislead those truly seeking You. Deliver us from ourselves O God, that we may embrace You with truly repentant hearts and turn away from our sins and traditions that honor men and leave us unholy and unworthy vessels for Your use. Remake the stony hearts in Your Church into hearts of flesh warm with Your love. Cleanse the filth of our ways so that we can see Your face and live; that we can hear Your voice and obey; that we can boldly speak out the proclamation of Your truth so that our lives lovingly express truth in all things: speaking truly, dealing truly, thinking truly, and living truly as honorable servants of our God. Enfolded in Your love O God, lead us and guide us to grow up in every way and in all things into Him who is the Head, even Christ, the Messiah, the Anointed One. Because of Him, the whole Body, Your Church, is closely joined and firmly knitted together by the joints and ligaments with which it is supplied, when each part is working properly and grows to full maturity and potential building itself up in love.

For this cause, I solemnly proclaim, that We, Your Church must no longer live as heathen in perverseness (sin, folly, vanity, emptiness of our souls and in futility of our own minds). Father, open our ears that we can hear Your proclamations of truth and hearken our understanding to repent of any and all darkened moral understanding and actions, so that we are enlightened and our clouded reasoning clears; so that We stand acceptable in Your sight for reconciliation and leading by Your Holy Spirit, with softened, repentant and contrite hearts, renewed with feverous sensitivity in our morals and conduct.

Stir up O God, our initial nature that You intended in the Garden of Eden, which has been corrupted since the Fall through lusts and delusions of earthly and carnal desires. Constantly renew our being, Father, in the spirit of our mind having a fresh mental and spiritual attitude fit for the uniting with our new nature in Your likeness. Heighten our awareness and discernment and purify our hearts, so we leave no foothold for our enemy. Grant us faithful feet that seek to walk following Your Son, Jesus. In His Name we pray. Amen.

Invitation

I lay in the grave of the damp, dark, and cold sodden earth. Ironically, the earth from which I was created now sucked the heat from deep within my bones. There was no casket around me – at least from my viewpoint. I knew neither pain nor fear as I returned to my origin of dust. The flesh that lay there in that hole facing the heavens, knew it could not rise forth. People above prayed and sang in an indescribable harmony. This was the first inclination I had that this was a funeral. The words they sang – I knew were the Word of God and they heightened the awareness of my soul still within its fleshly borders. At the end of the songs and prayers I heard the preacher say "Amen!" Immediately, dirt began falling on my face – one shovel full at a time. Only my eyes, ears, and lips could sense it though; my skin felt nothing as I laid in total absolute PEACE. As the hole filled, my spirit rose from the deep as a cloud rolling up a mountain after the heat of the day. My spirit hovered over the grave ever so briefly at what seemed to be 25 feet above the earth. Then looking to the heavens, my arms reaching upward to their fullest extension, I began seeing the Kingdom of God unveiled in the heavenlies. My new home –Jerusalem. I saw the City Wall towering above me. Shalom, shalom Jerusalem – the Home of Adonai.

The brown stone wall drew near me. I don't know which was moving, the wall or me, for I sensed no motion myself, yet the city manifested itself and fast-forwarded towards me until it cast a shadow alongside my new being and reclined somewhere above it. In the blink of an eye, I saw the Temple through the city and saw the towering pieces of a crimson red and purple curtain surrounding the Holy of Holies rent from top to bottom. I then heard a choir of voices proclaiming, "Heaven and Earth are filled with Your Glory O Lord! Hosanna in the Highest! Blessed is He who comes in the Name of the Lord." As the voices praised, the curtains swayed and danced as sheets in a breeze – and I knew the presence of God stirred it so.

Then in an instant, darkness enveloped me and I returned to the grave with the ground trembling as with birth pangs – awakening by the processional power of God in a brilliant white light in an unbridled, unveiled love. Too bright for eyes to behold, I shielded my face. The rays penetrated everything as if it were not even there. The face of God passed by though I didn't see it; I just knew that's what it was. His presence covered me and then passed through my being with indescribable warmth and knowing. I tried to rise and follow but He placed His hand upon my forehead and crown and softly spoke to my spirit in an otherwise inaudible voice, "My Spirit will lead you, but for now, you rest." When I opened my eyes, I could see sunrays from the heavens free from cloud interference. I was at the floor of the altar, prostrate in the presence of God – changed in ways I had not words for, other than refreshed, invigorated, and at total peace – and perhaps for the first time – really alive.

Jerusalem

Come quickly – Come quickly
Come quickly Lord Jesus
Come quickly – Come quickly
King of Israel!

Jerusalem, Jerusalem
Your people long for peace
O Jerusalem, Jerusalem
God hears your pleas
And the day will come
When our eyes will behold
The New Jerusalem unfolded
Jerusalem, Jerusalem
City on a hill
Jerusalem, Jerusalem
God will bless you still.

Jerusalem, Jerusalem
City on a hill
Jerusalem, Jerusalem
Your Temple He will fill
A glorious city you will be
When that day is come
As revealed in God's Word
Your day of Victory
O New Jerusalem
The eternal throne of our King!

Come quickly – Come quickly
Come quickly Lord Jesus
Come quickly – Come quickly
King of Israel!

Jesus, I Need You

I lived my life just how I wanted
Came and went as I pleased
But as I traveled on, the meaning of life was gone
And my choices didn't satisfy.

One night, I picked up that Bible
Polished clean, but unread
Flipping through pages, I read of sacrifices
And wondered what it all meant.

Then I crossed the book of Matthew
Where Jesus told Peter to follow Him
And He would make him a fisher of men
And in my heart, I heard Him speaking to me.

That night I asked Jesus to come into my heart
To forgive all my sins and turn me around.
Now I'm free with His Spirit living in me
His grace brought a new day where love abounds.

Friends, today the invitation remains the same
Will you open your heart to Him?
It's all really very simple
Just surrender your will and leave the rest up to Him.

Jesus I need you as my Savior
I confess all my sins
I'm tired of living my way
I come to You in faith, teach me how to live.

Jesus the Healer

Have you heard the news of the healer
Jesus of Galilee
The deaf now hear
and the blind, now they see
Even those who touch Him
change to perfectly whole.

I've got to reach Him
That healer from Galilee
My life seems broken beyond repair
My sin is too much for me to bear
I'll do anything just to be free
And if I touch Him, He will change me.

So what do I know about this Jesus
The Son of Man and Son of God?
I reached out my hand
And as His eyes fixed upon me
They burned with flames of love
He cleansed my spirit and I knew I was whole.

Just Wait

Set aside your cares and frustrations
Anxieties and confusion
Set aside the duties of the day
And all of life's decisions
Set aside your sins and shortcomings
And whatever else keeps you from Me
And come boldly before My throne
And just wait.

Come boldly before My throne of grace
Wait for Me with expectation and faith
Wait for Me there with confidence
My love wait for Me there with great joy
But most importantly,
Just wait.

Wait in peace and enjoy My rest
Wait for Me and I'll give you strength
Wait for Me, My love, My precious one
O eye of My creation
Reason for My salvation
Just wait.

You'll find nothing more important
Than this quiet time with Me
Offer the fruit of your faith
at My feet
Nothing else shall restore your soul
As this time you
Wait for Me.

When you think you're not seeing
When you think you can't hear
Stop believing what you're thinking
Quiet your mind and draw near
Closer and closer still
And wait.

Ask to see with My eyes
Ask to hear with My ears
Ask to feel with the touch of My hands
Ask for peace to calm your fears
And it shall be so
When you wait.

I ask you to wait
Because My thoughts and ways
Are higher than your own
I ask you to wait
To bring comfort to your soul
I ask you to wait
To gaze on the glory of My throne.

Stay a minute or an hour
A day, week, or year
And if you love Me
Stay a lifetime
And know I am here.

You'll hear the songs of angels sing
And the songs I sing to you
You'll see the love burn in My eyes
And feel Me gently stroke your hair
Safe will you remain, without a care.

You'll know I love you forever
And I'll dance with you here
I am faithful and appoint you
You will know that I anoint you
And I'll tell you the secrets of My heart
If you will,
Just wait.

<u>Justice</u>

DEPRAVITY
So selfish
So ungrateful
So crude
Fire of passion uncontrolled
Destroyer of the Gardens' sod
Mafia of man's soul
Ye shall NOT have the final breath
But shall lose to Holy wrath
In man's account to God.

__Kingdom Creed__

I am a redeemed child of God. I will not surrender to the enemy of my own free will. If I become lost in enemy territory, I will do all within my power to evade my captors. If found and taken captive, I will not rest in his prison. I will not accept favors from the enemy, or believe any of his lies. I will seek to restore unity with my brothers. I will devise a plan of escape with them. I will not turn against my own. I will seek every opportunity of escape without ceasing my efforts until the opportune time avails itself. I will not rest until my fellow captives and I are free. I choose to be punished for maintaining my righteous allegiances and die fighting for the faith I believe in rather than siding with the enemy or ever giving up the fight. I am a redeemed child of the King. Amen.

Lamentation

Lord forgive me
I denied You today
When I should I have grieved
by what I heard them say.
Instead, I laughed with the world
as they mocked Your grace
And now a cloud of darkness
veils my face.

I've since asked why and how
I could do such a thing
And I've only poor excuses
which now leave such a sting.
Lord I thought I was more faithful
than to do what I did today
But regardless,
the choices I've made stay.

Humble my heart, Lord
melt my fears and pride
Touch me with Your power.
Come again and abide.
Open my eyes, Father
to see Jesus as You do;
So that I will not make light
of the suffering
He went through.

Lasciviousness

Meditation: Galatians 5:13

Using liberty as an occasion of sin
I see the shadows
Without and within
The unholy angel dust doth glitter
In final preparation
To declare war
On the imagination.
While lifting off the flight deck
The enemy delights
For one of two
Will not come back tonight.
Totally deceived
Full throttle ahead
The ecstasy tailspins
And a friend is dead.
Trapped by the rubble
In shock one cries
Attempting to revive the other
Destroyed by the angels' lies
The victim shakes and weeps fully aware
Of the deception
That brought them there
And that shrouds
The angels' darkened faces.

Last Days

Sweet Fragrance
Whispering peace
Waving overhead
Far Reaching
Penetrating
Soaking heavy dew

May our worship
Rise in boldness
With full confidence
Of the love You bestow on us
Tears from faces
Held like pearls in Your hands

Bushes burning
Cherubs praising
Angels wrestling with men
Children dancing
Creation singing
Prophets prostrate in the sand

Trumpets blowing
Church walls falling
Eastern sky tearing
As the Lord descends
Come up here – Come up now
Let the reign begin

Sweet Fragrance
Whispering power
Sheep and grains of wheat
Ascending in the clouds
Love's reward
Forever without end.

Lessons from the Mail Room

In the mailroom, when it comes to forwarding mail, there are two classes. One has been paid to be forwarded and the other has not. Mail paid to be forwarded is sent to the new address. The mail not paid for is thrown away.

So think for a moment if you will, about your spiritual mail. If you have been born again, you have a new address on Righteous Road in the Glory subdivision; if not you live on Unregenerate Avenue. So when we are born again, it is as though we have moved to a new residence. Our thoughts however still go to the same old Post Office(our brain) for sorting, but the delivery address is different. The mail paid for (not with money but with the blood of Jesus) is forwarded. This mail is our Godly thoughts; that which are from God. But like any mail, after it is delivered it must be picked up or it just sits in the box worthlessly. Picking up the mail means opening, reading, and responding appropriately. In other words, the Bible must be opened, read and lived to be active.

But what of that old mail which has not been paid to be forwarded? It lacks the forwarding mark. It is considered worthless and tossed in the waste can. Likewise, God does not intend for us to receive the "Junk" mail (ungodly thoughts and beliefs) at our new address. Such are not from the Father and not paid for to be forwarded and are to be trashed. We would do well to train our mind to sort these thoughts just as our mail carrier does our mail. Thoughts from God are forwarded since the blood of the Lamb paid for them. The blood acts as our cancelled sin stamp. What of the ungodly thoughts, the Junk mail? It is to be trashed (rebuked, cast down, cast out, not accepted, not believed, renounced or otherwise rejected). The junk does not belong at the new address.

Have you moved to your new spiritual home in the land of the Lord? Is your mailbox clearly marked so you can receive your deliveries? Do you check that box daily like you do the mailbox by your house? You need not be afraid to go there. There is no junk mail waiting for you there. It has been cast out and is waiting to be burned if you are thinking with a renewed mind. Go to your box and open the important mail. Take possession of what is rightfully yours and act on it.

Let the Redeemed So Speak

Meditation: Psalms 107:2

Before men, let me proclaim the Word of the Lord!!
Let me keep silent only in the presence of His Holiness
While He speaks to His servant
That I may hear His instruction
To perform His perfect will.

Let the Words of the Lord be written within my heart
That He may use my mouth and hand to proclaim His will.
His words will not be hidden or kept silent
Lest the rocks begin to shout;
Nor shall they be sent out in vain and return void!
May the Word of the Lord:
Guide my ears...
My heart...
My hands...
My feet...
And my thoughts...
All the days of my life
Now and forevermore
Let my voice shout forth:
"Though my shackles seem as chains
The word of God speaks
And angels carry them away!"

<u>Life</u>

The earth shakes, quakes and trembles
Awaiting Your return
When she will
Rejoice in Your presence
And open embrace.

Oh Master
Almighty God
Prince of Peace
Let me be as the earth
Longing for You.

Forbid me be unyielding
To Your flow and heights
That You desire for my life
In service to You.

Burst through
All hardness of my heart
Til we dance as one.

I am Your earthen vessel
Moved by Your Spirit
As a mighty rushing wind
Purified by fire
Eager to walk with You
Across the Red Seas of life.

May the words of my mouth
And the meditations of my heart
Be pleasing to You
O God, my strength and my redeemer.

May the blessings of peace
And shouts of joy
Resound on this Holy ground
And continually seal our union. Amen.

Light of Glory

[SEED]
Small substance
Concealed in hardened shell
Insignificant to untrained eyes
With great potential
Fruitful harvest
If buried and dies

[CREATION – EARTH]
Spoken Word
Order from chaos
Magnificent universe
Ever increasing
Never ceasing
Hear creation sing

[CREATION – MAN]
Breath of life
Creative power of God
Hidden mystery
Treasure breathed
Into man's dust
So he comes alive

[JESUS]
Seed of Faith
Word of God
Babe in Mary's arms
Who would have thought
To place this jewel
In stony barren soil
That if dead would come alive again

[SALVATION]
Harvest seed
Penetrating hardened hearts
The dirt of sin from Eden days
Heart of stone into flesh
Transforming miracle
God indwelling man
Life defeats death again.

[REIGN]
More beautiful in perfect light
Extending to the heavens bright
Grace's fragrance sings
Now priests and kings
Light of Glory shine
Rapture's transforming rhyme.

CHORUS:
And life defeats death again
Death has lost its sting
The dead break forth from the ground
The light of glory reigns
The light of glory reigns!

Longings

I long for Your heart
Your eyes
Your touch
Your compassion
Your kind of love in me.

I've looked many places
Right and wrong
Hoping and longing for
What only comes from You.

I don't know why
I looked for You
In the faces of others
And the riches of this world.

And while I was looking
All the places I thought I'd find You
I refused to surrender
To let You do what I never could.

All that time
When I was so far away
I just never knew
You were right here at my side.

Waiting
Just waiting
Waiting
For me to hear
You finished all the work
And were waiting
For me to receive.

Put my agenda aside
Lay down my pride
And receive You
Conceding I was clay
Quit insisting on my own way
And receive You
O how I complicated
Your simple truth
To receive You.

All that striving
All the wasted time
When all there was left for me to do
Was receive You.

Waiting
Just waiting
Waiting
For me to hear
You finished all the work
And were waiting
For me to receive You.

Now I hear
No longer deaf and blind
I receive you
I receive you
Jesus
I receive you.

Love Offering

Lord I give You my all
Not knowing now what all that may be,
But I know from days past
My all is all I have to give.

You can take my scraps of offerings
Bless them 10,000 fold,
Make blessings far beyond
What I could ever imagine,
That's why I give You my all.

I give You all of my joy
Because You first loved me.
I give You obedience in love
For You are the only true and just God.
I give You my fragile frame
You know I'm formed from dust,
But You grant me to be a son
And teach me to trust.

I give You my sorrow,
I've nowhere else to go.
And You dry every tear
And free me from every fear,
Teaching me to believe
I'm safe in Your arms.

I know if I give You my all
Not knowing what that might be,
You will hold me safe in Your hands
Even though the enemy encamps.
You tell me his realities are lies
Fictitious distortions of truth
And in You alone I can trust
So I give you my all.

And tomorrow, I'll do it again
'Til there's no more of them.
And if I fall, I won't run away.
I'll get up again and call Your Name.
'Til I see You face to face,
I give You my all.

Lullaby

Daddy
I'm so glad that You are here.
In Your lap,
I've Your eye and ear.
Secure in Your arms
I've peace in my soul
From Your gentle touch
And secure embrace
I've a love greater
Than words I know.

Eyes sparkling
When twain doth meet
My every doubt fading
As I sit at Your feet
My faults though many
Forgiven and cleansed
My steps You carefully order
So I don't trip and fall again.
Yet when I don't listen
I trip and fall on my face,
But even then You don't forsake me
You reach to take my hand
And help me up again.

Rock me again
In your arms of love
Dry each tear I cry
And as I sleep
Sing to me another
Comforting lullaby.

Mary Magdalene's Song

Shortcomings and shame
Tugged on my soul
Until I froze in doubt and fear
When sin walked in my mind's door
Taking me captive to its will
And convinced me
I was unacceptable.

For years I hid
Behind shields of lies
While sin ate away
My momentum and pride
The righteous scoffed and mocked me
Called me names of shame
But nothing changed me
And I continued on my way.

Then I met You
I remember well the hour
When caught in sin
I was cast out in the open
For all to see and scorn.

And they picked up stones to kill me
By the Law they had the right
But You who were sinless
Wrote in the sand
And my accusers
From old to young disappeared.

Filled with fear
And jubilant wonder
I heard You call my name.
You knew all about me
My wretchedness and depths of sin
And knew I wasn't worthy,
Yet me You did not condemn.

When I heard You say my name
That no one had told You
I looked up from Your feet
To see the one who
Knew so much about me,
Then instead of accusations
You reached for my hand
And such love
Flowed from Your eyes.

Such kindness and mercy
I had never known
And have never
Been able to forget.
How You so worthy and without sin
One who had right to judge me
Gave another chance
And loved me enough
To help me to my feet again.

How can I not love You?
How can I not sing?
For when I was nothing
You gave me everything.

Mighty Warrior

O the mighty power of prayer
Charging force of light
Expeller of darkness
Conqueror of night
Exposer of sins and secrets
Driver of Satan to flight.

O the mighty power of prayer
Strong and faithful shield
Marching ever onward
Impeding darts of evil
Shatterer of strongholds
Shackle breaker with surrendered will.

O mighty power of prayer
Sweet grace so undeserved
Redeeming sinners to heirs
Power to soften the hardest stone
Into a heart of flesh
Salvation come to sinful flesh
Rewarder of obedience.

More of Your Power Lord

More of Your power Lord
I long to know
More authority
than I've ever known
Not for my own glory Lord
But rather to show
You are real
to those humbled before You
believing You heal.

I open my vessel
Come fill and cleanse deep within.
Take a flaming coal from Your altar
and burn away
all of my iniquity and shame.
Purify my heart until
it is one with Yours
Lift my head and fix my eyes
anoint my soul and heart
with Your perfect sight.

More Questions

Why do I feel so alone
In storm clouds dark
And rain so cold
With lightning flashes
As the thunder rolls?

Why is it I feel afraid
Tension increasing with perceived pain
Raging emotions succumbing to hate
Like seemingly controlled by unpredictable fate.
Should I go on or rest my case?

Why is it I feel I cannot go home
To the place I once desired to go
To rid myself of sorrows and woe
Is a place once so loved – now a foe?
I'm left standing alone – freezing in the cold.

Why it is I can't make peace
With my God or the untamable Beast
The battle shall never cease
Until...I pray on bended knee
My questions will unanswered be.

My Beloved

O to be known
For all my faults and sins
Nakedly exposed
And not cast away
But gently gathered in.

O what loving friend
Could there ever be
In Heaven or on earth
To gaze upon all ugliness
Yet want to cleave to me?

What songs of praise
Does nature speak
Of this boundless love?
What of the morning sky's radiance
That shines on all from above?

Sing ye heavens above
And earth below
Of God's love for man
The crucified Son of God
The perfect sacrificial lamb!

No sin, shame or pride can dwell
In this Holy place
Where scarlet stain is cleansed
From red to white
Where untainted blood eradicates sin.

Naked now and fully known
Yet without fear or shame
I know my Savior's endless love
As I behold His face
As the recipient of His redeeming grace.

Hear O hearts of every land
The love of God for man
All glory to the Risen One
Who knows my frame of dust
Yet passionately whispers my name.

My Love

Arise My love, arise My love
Take to the temple your sacrifice
I will meet you there at the altar
And spill My blood for your life.

Come away, come away My love
Come with Me into My fields
Let us behold in adoration
The harvest we will reap.

Hear My voice, hear My voice My love
Feel My arms hold you tight
You are My beloved
I will not leave your side.

I'm coming soon, I am coming soon
Riding on the eastern sky
But until the time that I should come
Tend My sheep and draw them nigh.

My Spirit Cries

I stand at the brink of a great crevasse;
My life before me and past behind
Has my path ended or just begun?
Faced with retreat or a courageous jump
I ponder life bringing me here
Is it a plan or fate?
Tomorrow's outcomes press cumbersomely on my brow
And I seek tomorrow's wisdom now.
If this crossing is my fate,
To this place I'll return
Again and again until I've learned.
With little doubt and full of fear
I know a new life waits beyond this frontier.
Yet, I've not the strength in my own flesh.
If I leap alone, I will surely crash!
Out of fear, desperation, and hope MY SPIRIT
CRIES...
As I leap toward Heaven and unknown skies.

Mystery

I've often wondered
How You created
Everything by a spoken word

I'm always amazed
At the beauty You designed
As home for man

And I've tried to conceive
How You could leave
Your throne for me

That's more love
Than I understand
More love
Than I've ever known

To leave a throne
The splendor of heaven
To be born a babe
And to die a sacrifice

I don't know how
You restrained Yourself
When You were lied about
And spat on

How You took the beating
For my healing
The nails and pain

When You could have spoken
Just one word
And angels come and carry You away.

That's more love
Than I understand
More love
Than I've ever known

That's more obedience
Than I've ever known
More love and compassion
Than a sinner is worthy of

That's more mercy
Than I could ever imagine,
Dream or think

That's more grace and more faith
Than any of us here could ever know
But for the love of God.

So how do I ever thank you?
How do I ever thank You,
But love those You love?

Nakedness

I have dared to seek and see
What my sin looks like to You, O God
I have glimpsed upon the fire of Your anger
        In days of Old
The brokenness of Your heart
And tears in Your eyes
        In days present
And the shed blood of Your mercy.

I have seen my flesh
And the carnality of my mind
For what it is
Wretched, stinking and pitiful
No match before a Holy God.

When I read in Your Word
Of Adam and Eve,
I marvel at their fear and hiding
My heart cries for them to run to
And not away from You,
In repentance while renouncing their sin.
Yet I know no man is different today.

We still attempt to hide our secrets
From You and others
Just as Adam and Eve.
We are guilty of exercising license to sin
And cheapen the grace You have bestowed upon us
As we continue in our rebelliousness
As Satan did himself
Without ever seeing Your heart in our sin.
By hiding truth we hide ourselves
From Your justice, truth, mercy, and forgiveness.

As a result, I confess this as sin
And renounce my ways
And ask for You to forgive me
For struggling against You.
Cleanse my heart again
O righteous lover of my soul
Instill Your statues and love
In this hardened and unreceptive heart of mine
Until it transforms my heart to a life
Unable to beat without You.
Keep me O God
From following the twisted path of my emotions
Instead of the peace of Your embrace.
Discipline me Father, as a beloved son
Search and reveal to me my ambitions and desires
So the words of my mouth and the meditations of my
heart
Are pleasing to You, O Holy Father.
Extinguish the bastardly lies of my ugliness and
unwantedness
I hear the mouths of men that stand against Your Holy
Order.
Instill in me the desire to receive Your acceptance
As supreme over the words of men.

Teach me blessed Father
To follow Your example
Of Your anointed son, Jesus Christ
Who met people where they were
In their humanity
But saw them with the eyes of God
And Loved unselfishly.

Nature's Testimony

The tree branches sway
Giving You praise.
The amber waves of grain
Proclaim Your beauty and abundance.
The sun burns faithfully
Shining dimly compared to Your glory.
The moon lights the darkest night
As Jesus' words of salvation's grace.
Flowers bloom in the morning
Unveiling their beauty
And bow their head at night
In honorable duty.
The tides rise and fall
By Your precise design
Yet men do the same
Without discerning the times.
The earth shouts its praise to You
While men in Your image remain mournfully silent
O Soul of Man
If you would hear nature's cry
Your beauty would unfold in splendor,
If you would but humble yourself
Forsake your wicked ways and pray.
Yes, pray O man
Seek the face
Of the Creator of all.
Dip your robe
In His crimson grace,
Then behold the wonder of sin washing away,
Purifying your heart,
As you fix your gaze
Upon Him.

New Covenant

In just a while
I will shake the heavens
I will shake the earth and sea
Dry lands will tremble
And the seas tsunami
As will all the nations
And all that will
Shall come to me.

And in those days
I will fill this house with glory
The silver is mine
As is the gold
And the glory of my new house
Shall be greater than that of old.
In this place is peace and blessing
Open arms of love.
Neglect not the words of the prophets
Or of My own Son.

New Song

I feel like dancing
I feel like singing
I feel like praising the Lord
He reached down and saved me
And I'm no longer under
The power of the enemy
That's why I'm praising the Lord

I once was bound in sin
Chained to the ground from within
My hope caving in around
I was hell bound
On a one way train down
Thought no one knew or cared
Until I saw the love in His eyes

Ask me why I dance
Ask me why I sing
I'll gladly tell you
About my mighty King
Jesus my Savior
The redeemer who took my place
O what love and grace

Now I'm dancing
And now I'm singing
Jesus, sweet Jesus
How I love that Name
No other power
Could heal and make me whole
'Til He came to lead me home.

O Precious Child

O Precious Child
Sleep in My arms.
I take all cares and sorrows away.
Your fruit is sweet and pleasing to My taste,
I delight in the offering you've given.
You have brought forth seed entrusted to you
Rest in My arms now, for a season.
My left hand steadies your head
And My right embraces you.

I see your face shining
As it will in the day you come to Me
And your face is lovely.
I hear your voice
a refreshing sound to my ears
You are so beautiful

O beloved, precious one
I am your strength
I am your song
And you, the gold for which I have longed
A true reflection
Of the glory of God.

Ode to the Creator

Bring order to my chaos
Creator of heavens and earth
My soul – formless and void
Longs for Your Divine Word.
Speak light into my darkness
With Your facets of Glory shine
Melt my heart of stone
'Til with You, I'm aligned.

Hold back the flood
That threatens to swallow my soul
Make for me a firmament
A finely sculptured wall
To hold raging tides at bay
Lest I perish at their surge
Deliver me from evil
With Thy Holy embrace.

Confine the tempest
And his sea billows' roll
Transforming the mud
Of my murky soul
To fertile ground –
Rich, yielding soil.

Bring forth vegetation
In the field of my life
With seeds reproducing
After their own kind
Trees of fruitful harvest
In which reapers delight.

May Your Spirit be my Light
And I as the universe
Held in position
By Your mighty power
All the seasons of my years
Walking with You by day
Then through fearless night.

Create a place for me
With Your other creatures
So a balanced world we share
Whether mighty beast
Or creeping thing
Guide me to their tender care.

Draw me nearer yet
O God above the earth
Breathe Your breath
Into my dust
So I become a living soul
Created in Your image
An extension of Your own
With authority to take dominion
And the will to obey.

With Your creation complete
Teach me to Rest
To gaze upon Your beauty
And know it is Good
So all is well with my soul.
Blessed be the Sabbath
I am whole!

Open Heaven

Pine needles cover the forest floor
A thatched roof for another world
Insects, centipedes, and furry moss
Creep through the carpet's morning frost

Up and down stairs
In and out many doors
A world its own 'neath layered floor.
The sky above both worlds below
Each contending for radiant flow,
With the intellectual oft unaware
What is disturbed by his glaring stare.
He is less like God
Than he dare believe,
Hibernating in the frozen seasons of life
When once he ate berries in broad daylight,
No dreams of roaming the third heaven of earth's delight

While above the third heaven
The fourth heaven,
Where the heaven of earth sings,
Bringing sunlight, cloud, wind and needed rain.
Eyes ever gazing to the true Heaven above
A praiseworthy beauty not often enough sang of.

While back at pine needles on the floor
As far as eyes can see
Trees raise their branches high above
An unspoken praise to their God.
The shade a holy benediction to that below
A twofold mission,
Magnifying God and protecting creation,
Servant and master
With shelter and shade.

From my feet to the highest peak
From left to right
Encircling and enfolding the weak,
My weary soul now rests in peace
In the secret place
of which I speak.

Passages

Meditations:
Proverbs 22:6
Mark 10:14-15
Matthew 10:28

The boy plays contently in the meadow
with his cars and trucks
making roads and mud pits
sometimes feeding ducks.
Not a worry…not a care
All his needs provided there.
Love and joy fill his days
The Father's love not in vain.

He sees her sitting in peripheral view
two rows over in history class
He ponders the wonder in his heart
for this one is so different.
She becomes the beauty
         his eyes behold…
Cars and trucks traded away
For the mystery of love
And walks along the bay.

The boy looks over the meadow
         while mine sweepers
         defuse death before dawn
The desolate battlefield
         inundated with terror
         ages him beyond his years;
The days of youth – ancient now
As sweat beads upon his brow.

Tension mounts as troops advance
Hind's feet is salvation here
Death's tolling bell a creepy sneer
Mines and traps dare his steps
With danger undetectable to the eye
Senses sharpen
To protect his soul
And guard his life.

Friends once near...
Now so far...
Lost forever to the damnation of the war.
The man's heart grieves and laments
Wretched doubt and agony surmount
Forty days and forty nights...
The playing fields out of sight
When
Silently...
Creeping...
Just before the dawn
The memory FLASHES
And takes him back
To cars...
Trucks...
And feeding ducks,
In the meadow out back.

Perfect Love

I stood broken and weak before You
And in desperation bared my soul.
You embraced me gently and kissed my forehead
And prayed the Father make me whole.

For this I love and treasure You
In more ways than words I know.
For loving me broken
While You restored my soul.

Perfect lover of my soul
I adore You
Pure, undefiled, healing love
That ever draws me near
Dries my every tear
Calms all my fears
In Your presence, all doubt disappears
And I adore You
I adore You
Perfect Love.

Petitions

Shine light on my blindness
The pride that looks at outward man
While forgetting that You look within.
In spite of imperfections
You place treasure therein,
We each with a calling
More souls to win.

Open my deaf ears, Lord
That only appear to care
Because though hearing
My thoughts are not there.
Tune my ears to hear You
To more than words said
To guide and encourage
Those oppressed by men.

I cry out wholeheartedly
Help me O Lord!
I long to keep Your statutes
And can't do it without You.

Hold my tongue
When it speaks too soon
Without thinking first
What You would say or do.
Sift my careless words
Incinerate them with Your fire
So I walk in Your desires.

I confess my attitude
Too often is not right,
I'm more concerned about myself
Than others at my side.
Renew a right spirit
Deep within my heart
Wash away all of my pride,
Make me a blessing
More compassionate and kind.

Please Show Me

Please show me the love of Jesus
I need to see the compassion in His eyes
Please show me His loving kindness
I want to see through such loving eyes.

I've wasted years chasing rainbows
Just to find there's no gold at the end
I've tried all I know to win God's favor
Just to learn He's no respecter of men.

It's hard for me to confide in others
Just when I need them, they let me down
I've traded hope for all life's pleasures
Just to learn they never satisfy.

Please show me the love of Jesus
I need to see the compassion in those eyes
I've no hope left for tomorrow
I need Him now, I've no where else to go.

Please, someone show me the love of Jesus
I need to know there's love in His eyes
I stand here guilty of betrayal
I need to know He'll dry the tears I cry.

Please show me the love of Jesus
My careless walk left me blind
Please show me His compassion
I need His touch to restore my sight.

Pour It In

Pour in
Pour in
Pour in Your love
Pour it in
Pour it in

Expand our temple dwellings
        to receive more of Your love.
Thy Kingdom come dearest Lord
        Thy will be done.
Increase our borders Lord
        that Your hand be with us.
Keep us from
Keep us from
Keep us from the Evil One.

Bring this land Your healing
        as we humble ourselves.
We turn Lord, we turn now
        from our wicked ways;
Seeking only You
        and the glory of Your face.
Teach us to pray, O Lord
        to know Your will
and Your way.
Mold us, Your vessels
        And as we yield
remake us like You.
Sensitize our ears and eyes
        so in Your Spirit we move.

Let all hearts cry out
        the holiness of Your Name.
Bowing before
        Your throne of grace,
Knowing our life is not our own
        but one for whom Jesus paid.
Praise, honor, and glory
        the angels sing…
Praise, honor, and glory
        let the earth proclaim…
Holy, Holy, Holy
        Holy is Your Name.

Come Alpha and Omega
        Bright and Morning Star,
Come root and Son of David
        exalted now on High.
Come quickly
Come quickly
Come quickly Lord Jesus
We long for You.

Pour in
Pour in
Pour in Your love
Pour it in
Pour it in
Come quickly
Come quickly
Come quickly Lord Jesus
We long for You.

Pouring Rain

I come here to see Your face
And sing praises to Your Holy Name
My God, my provider, and friend
My God, my life within.

You wash me clean
That's why I stay
On this granite Rock today
Sitting in the pouring rain.

Why would I want to go away
When You are here with me always
To cleanse my soul
And heal me in Your Name?

You wash me clean
That's why I stay
On this granite Rock today
Sitting in the pouring rain.

Dear Lord
Pour down Your rain.

Praise and Sing

Thank You, O Lord Most High
Shout joyfully, O my soul
Enlarge the gladness of my service
So that I stand continually before You
Singing and dancing full of joy.

I know, O Lord, You are my God and Creator
That even from before the womb
      You knew me
You created me with divine purpose
To protect Your own
As a shepherd, his sheep.

Teach me, O Lord, how to offer
The praise and thanksgiving You deserve
I bless You and sing of Your goodness
I know You hear my humble cries;
Your loving kindness is everlasting
And Your faithfulness endures evermore.

      Sing O Sing
      Body, soul and spirit
      Exalt the Lord
      Rejoice
      Magnify!

Praise Him

Praise Him
You sun, moon and bright shining stars
Praise Him
You angels and heavenly hosts
Let the whole creation
Praise Him

Praise Him You heavens
And all that's above
Praise Him You earth
And all that's below
Praise Him
Praise Him

Great in power
Great in glory
Great in wonder
King of Heaven
Great in Zion
King over all
Only You are worthy
To be praised.

Praise You

Praise You...Praise You
O I gotta praise You.

Praise You in the morning when I rise
Singing Glory Hallelujah
Father, Creator – giver of life.

Make me like David in the courtyard
Dancing and singing – I cannot keep quiet
Jesus, my Savior brings me light.

Majestic mountains sing Your Name
Mighty rivers with cleansing power
Flow down from Your throne on High.

I'll sing Your praises all my life
Singing Glory Hallelujah
I'm a child in Your image who reflects Your light.

I abide in the shadow of Your wings
A priest and king through Jesus Christ
Anointed to live and to love.

I'm the child of Your delight
Eternal Father giver of the Spirit
Living Water – song of my heart.

Worship in song
Worship in dance
Crash the cymbals
Blow the shofar!

Praise You....Praise You
O I gotta Praise You!!
PRAISE YOU!!!

Prayer and Obedience

I said, I love you, Lord.
> He said, "Forbid not the little ones
> And go feed my sheep."
I repeated again, I love you, Lord.
> "Hear then My voice
> and go heal the sick."
You know I love you, Lord.
> "Go into all the world
> Teach My Word to every land."
O, I love you, Lord.
> "He who loves Me
> hears and obeys."

<u>Prayer of Restoration</u>

Lord, I cry to You in the midst of my despair. My heart breaks when I forsake Your way even for a moment. You are my Rock, O Mighty One, my shelter from temptation and evil that seek to draw me away from You.

Forgive me, O Lord for straying from Your path of Righteousness by not fleeing to You in time of need and temptation. Grant Your servant quickened ears to hear Your voice above the voice of temptation and as Your sheep, to answer only to Your voice.

Restore me as only You can, Holy Father. Do not allow the guilt of my offenses to overtake me and pull me away from Your saving grace, forgiveness, and loving arms.

Bring to my remembrance Your promises as to who I am in Christ Jesus: the head and not the tail, the redeemed not the condemned, and the blessed not the cursed.

Set my eyes upon Your face, O God of my Salvation, and stay that gaze through my life in times of joy and success and in hardship and trials alike, so I may always behold Thy face's loving grace and continue on Your path of righteousness, victorious in You all of my days, through Jesus Christ my Lord. Amen.

Prayer Warrior

I have seen in young faces
      Battle scars from life
      Heavy burdens and worries
Confounding even the wise.

I have seen in these faces
      Despair, distrust, and lies
And I lift those precious souls to Thee
As I lie down my head each night.

Precious Child of Mine

There is a great cloud of witnesses above
And though I know they are there,
     I see them by faith, not by sight.
For those in Heaven, I am grateful
But there are so many here, too
     I see with earthly eyes;
Those with whom
     God knows He used to spare my life.

For each and every time
     you loved me just as I was
For teaching me
     about what you knew
For all the times
     you lifted me with your smile
For giving me the hope
     to make it through one more trial.

For all the times you told me
     "God is able,"
For every time you held me
     while I did nothing but cry
For every prayer of encouragement
     you spoke over me
And for giving me those moments of your time.

For all the times you said:
     "Your Daddy loves you."
For all the times
     You dried the tears from my eyes
For every prayer
     That we stood together in agreement
And for reminding me
     Who I was in our Father's eyes.

God has a word
for your obedience and compassion
He knows these require more of you
than simple sacrifice.
To you He says:

"Come and be blessed
for people see My Son in your eyes.
I am pleased with you
            and there's so much more of Me
            I desire to give to you.
Come and receive
            Come and rejoice with Me.
Come take in more of My Spirit,
Let Me fill your vessel
            Until you overflow.
You have proven trustworthy
            In guarding what is dear to Me below.
Come receive
Come rejoice with Me.
Precious,
Yes, you are precious,
O precious child of Mine."

<u>Prodigals</u>

Claps of thunder – rumbling earth
Manna quivers to the ground
Lightning strikes – winds roar
Wasting communion wine of our Lord
Such is depravity of sin
With which the carnal man whores.

Prophet Cry

I hear grieving cries
In lands far away
The sobbing and pain
Of hearts
Longing to be free.

I see in the faces
    Of those I pass each day
Masks hiding thoughts and feelings
    Protecting secrets
Of the longing to be free.

I see the prayers of the saints rising to the throne
    Like smoke from many fires
And tears gathered in buckets
    Like water from a well
Treasured in Heaven what is despised in Hell.

I see the animals listening intently
    To sounds men refuse to hear
I see them running to safety
Hearing the sound of the Lion of Judah
Roaring before He appears.

Shout and proclaim the Word, you Prophets!
Dancers bow and sway.
Singers lift your voice.
Intercessors pray.
Praise His Holy Name!

Speak in Spirit
Neglecting not truth and love.
Proclaim His grace and mercy,
Yet, be not silent of
The Judgment Day to come.

Open the eyes of man, O Lord
Tear the scales away
So we can gaze upon Your goodness
To prepare to draw near
Before the flame of time…
….flickers…
…. away.

Cleanse our hearts
O God of Heaven
To draw near
To You
To Join You
Live in You
No more us
Just You
'Til we are nothing
But
YOU.

Psalm of a Latter Day

Lord Jesus, You know my heart is heavy today. I long to spend time alone with You to praise You, yet it seems distractions steal the time away. My spirit craves to worship You in song, prayer, silence, and overflowing joy. My soul thirsts for the quenching only You offer in Your Holy Spirit. I know Your well of living water is present in this barren land of mine, for even right now it is a deep river flowing far beneath the surface. Life's daily demands draw me away from private intimate moments with You, but I know I am not abandoned. I see You, feel You, and hear You in my spirit, mind, heart and soul, yet I long for more. You speak to me in parables during my simple daily tasks so I can understand. In this I delight. Jesus, You have cared so affectionately and lovingly for me during those times when I was not affectionate or loving in return, neither to You or my fellow man.

How obvious is Your love for me!! I stand in awe of a love that reaches from holiness to sinfulness. Surely, it is more than my earthen mind can comprehend. O Lord Jesus forgive my shallowness of faith, imperfect following, and worldly distractedness. Instill in my heart as much love, gentleness, compassion, boldness, power, and joy as I can bear. I know in my spirit from Your written Word that my cup already overflows in abundance. Hear the praise of my spirit cry out in thanksgiving, honor, and glory to Your Holy Name, precious Jesus, for my words have not the power to articulate my thoughts.

I feel Your strength rushing below and beginning to rise to the surface as I awaken from the depths of my earthen ground. You break forth with the power of a geyser; bursting high and far beyond, as to envelope and energize my being. The earth quakes and trembles with Your passage until she rejoices in Your towering peak and returns still in Your open embrace. O Master, Almighty God, and Prince of Peace forbid me be unyielding to Your flow and heights You desire for my life in service to You. Burst through all the hardness of my heart 'til we dance as one in harmony with Your creation. For I Lord am Your vessel, moved by Your Holy Spirit as a rushing wind, purified by fire, and eager to walk with You across the River Jordan.

May the words of my mouth and the meditations of my heart be pleasing to You, O God, my strength and my redeemer. May the blessings of peace and shouts of joy that resound on this Holy ground continually refresh my soul with the confidence of the seal of our union. AMEN.

Psalm of Restoration and Hope

I hear the lies the enemy whispers
    seductively in my mind
    and begin to swerve and swagger
    as his trap door swings open wide.
I feel so weak captured in
    the invisible prison
    he detains me in
    and I weep in fear.
I know I must try to block my ears
    for my desire is only to hear
    the Spirit's truth
    and know not the fear
And though I feel God is far away
    I know such feelings lie
    and that my God is surely near
    even as tears flood my eyes.
So I arise from the pit of death
    that desires to strangle my faith
    and flee to a holy refuge
    where I know I'm safe.
Thank you Jesus for Your comfort
    in unconditional love
    from the body of Your Church
    that You died to establish and preserve.
Through Your faithful servants
    I can hear Your voice above
    the confusing noise
    and am amazed at Your indwelling love.
By the intercessory prayers
    of Your faithful ones
    I hear Your voice destroy the lies
    previously raging in my mind.
One by one as each lie
    tries to penetrate,
    Your Word overthrows the assailant
    by establishing the Word of Truth.

As the torrid battle ceases,
    all the torment, pain and tears
    which overshadowed my soul
    surrender to His word "Shalom."

Forgive me Lord for the weakness
    of my frail and doubting human frame
    and of my many actions
    that fall short of glorifying Your Name.

Father God, Almighty One, Holiest El Shaddai
    I confess my lack of faith and my will to die
    instead of remembering You
  and Your refuge on High.
Dearest Jehovah Jireh, Yahweh, Eloheim
    teach me, O merciful Father
    in courageous bold faith to cry out to You
    when the tempter's craftiness beguiles.
Holy, Holy, Holy Lord
    at Your feet I lay my crowns
    of pride, fear, and stubborn independence
    which erect the invisible prison
and seal my lips from praise.
In loving trust and surrender
    before You, I humbly bow
    laying all of my burdens
    and idolatrous crowns down.
Accept my prayers and confessions
    let my thanksgiving and praise arise
    as I covet Your peace and greatly yearn
    to see You and myself with Your Holy eyes.
Though I've no right of my own
to make such a request,
    I ask it in the Name of Your Son,
    my only hope now and forever
    interceding for His beloved.

It is in His Holy Name
        according to Your Word in John 17
        before the shedding of His sinless blood
        that He asked for our protection unity.

Thank you, Father God for forgiving my sins
        and quickening my spirit, body and soul
        so that I am receiving all the fullness
        of Your Divine love.

Of all that You were, and will ever be
        totally secure from the enemy
        no longer alone, but joined as one
throughout eternity
        I in You and You in me.
    Selah

Psalm of Rhema

I am an obedient child of God washed in the blood of the Lamb, Jesus Christ. I have been buried with Him in my confession of faith and in Christian baptism, raised to walk a new life as a new creation. My old man has passed away and all things are new. I have been born again into the Kingdom of God. As God's precious child, I stand in a position of righteousness – not by the works, which I have done, but by the finished work provided by God himself – Jesus on the cross. God himself has called me an heir, a child of His by which I can cry out Abba Father. As God's precious child, I am righteous in His sight though presently I am living in an imperfect, unglorified body. How amazing it is that He, the Holy God himself desires communion with a lower being. Yet, I know in the physical realm this is also true when parents love a child. Just as an infant finds nourishment and comfort as a suckling at the mother's breast, I earnestly desire to rest in the comfort of the Almighty arms protected and loved, a suckling of His breast. My very life comes forth from Him. Oh how I love Him and desire to be like Him! How I long for more of Him to be manifested in me.

Having this glorious mind of Christ, I do as He and meditate on the Word of God. I think on the Word and speak the Word. I choose for my thoughts and words to line up with the Word, so I am built up to DO the Word. I meditate on the Scriptures for truth, strength, perseverance, and discernment. My eyes, ears, and mouth are then opened to God's divine understanding. God and God alone is the strength of my heart and my portion forever.

The Word of God says in Joshua 1:8, "This book of the Law shall not depart out of thy mouth; but thou shalt meditate therein day and night that thou mayest observe to do according to all that is written therein. For then thou shalt make thy way prosperous and then thou shalt have good success." I affirm and declare that nothing in this present life compares to the riches He bestows upon me according to the riches of His glory. I receive ALL the promises my Father has decreed are mine according to His Word, right now.

The past, present, and future are all one entity to my God, though at this moment, I cannot comprehend such since I am presently bound to the frameworks of linear time. My God is not bound by such though, and I know that it is impossible for Him to lie and that He does not change according to Titus 1:2, Hebrews 6:18, Psalm 15:4, and Malachi 3:6. Because of this, I wait expectantly for the fulfillment of His promises even now. I confess all my doubts about His truths and ask forgiveness and for a greater trust in the measure of faith granted me. Thank you Lord for honoring my request.

Based on Your truth, I know that "the fear of the Lord is the beginning of wisdom" (Proverbs 9:10). I know Satan is a liar and there is no truth in him. He is the father of all lies and has been so from the beginning. With the mind of Christ given me, I carefully examine and discern all of my thoughts to see if they be from God, other men, the enemy, or myself. I do so to protect my body, soul, and spirit from deception knowing that my imaginations prompt and motivate my behavior according to Proverbs 23:7 which says, "As a man thinketh in his heart, so is he." My heart's desire is to love the Lord with all my being and love my neighbor as myself. In doing this, I surrender greater degrees of my humanity as the Lord leads.

I know that struggles and trials will come in this life. But I know from Ephesians 6:12 that I "do not struggle against flesh and blood, but against principalities, powers, and rulers of darkness of this world and spiritual wickedness in high places." This is why I suit myself with the whole armor of God and when I have done all I know to do I will continue to stand on the rock of my salvation, which cannot be moved. I am like the tree planted by the waters that shall not be moved because of my immovable foundation in Christ.

As a result of my assurance in Christ, when negative, guilt driving, condemning, or fearful thoughts emerge, I can choose to take action. I can forbid letting thoughts contrary to the Word of God enter and stay in my mind. I can cast down vain imaginations and bring them captive unto the obedience of Christ Jesus. When I am discouraged, I will fight the battle to praise my God, seek uplifting from the saints, and meditate on the Word of the Lord.

When I sin, by thought, word, or deed, by commission or omission, I will repent and be restored to fellowship by His merciful grace. Whether I am weak or strong, I will praise the Lord. Blessed be the Lord, the Head of the Body and blessed be the Body that submits itself to the Lord.

When challenges come my way, instead of seeing the defeat the enemy desires, I will proclaim victory and see the situation as God sees it! I will see myself victorious, whole, faithful, and overwhelmingly powerful by the strength of His right hand and my advocate Jesus. I boast not in myself; for I am simple flesh and bone, dust of the earth easily blown by the wind. I boast not in arrogance or for the praises of men, but rather to glorify the power of God in this earthen vessel that answers to the high calling of the Lord. I proclaim by His promises that I will rise above all circumstances to complete the journey of my high calling. I pray and exalt my God with understanding in my native tongue and in the tongues of angels to glorify my Father by the Holy Spirit's leading. I know at times I know not how to pray, but trust His leading to accomplish His perfect will. I yield my life to the ministry of the Gospel, graciously accepting my assignments thereof in obedience to God.

I meditate on His plans for my life and know He is faithful and just. I know He has cleansed me from all unrighteousness by the blood of Jesus. The life I now live, I live in the care of God Almighty, maker of Heaven and earth. The heavens and earth will one day be filled with the glory of my King.

Proclaim and praise His Holy Name. Praise the Father, Praise the Son, and Praise the Holy Spirit for the glory of the Lord is rising among us! Holy, Holy, Holy. Holy, Holy, Holy. Holy is the Lord God Almighty! Heaven and Earth are full of Thy Glory. Hosanna, Hosanna in the Highest. Blessed is He who comes, yes blessed is He who comes in the Name of the Lord! Hosanna in the Highest! Blessing and glory, and honor, power, and might be to our God forever and ever! HALLELUJAH – AMEN!!!!!!

Purpose

You are the goodness
That comes from my hands.
I am dry bones
Clay vessel of man.
You filled me with dirt
Put seeds in my hands,
I hold Your roots
Within my land.
You are the Living One
Unfolding in me
I take no credit
For the flower that grows.
I am the vessel
For the seeds You sow.

You are the tenderness
That reaches from my hands.
You are the compassion
And patience for every man.
You are the feet
Treading on when I would faint.
You are my beating heart
And the very breath I take.

I'm a useless pot collecting dust
Without Your soil and seeds.
You are my only goodness
All the marrow in my bones.
I give You permission to crush me
And remold me according to Your desire,
        the right vessel
For the seeds of Your heart.

You are the reason
For which I was born.
You are the bud
From me that springs forth.
I once was a formless
Broken vessel of a man,
Then you remade me
And planted Your seeds in my hands.

You are the reason
I bow my head and pray.
You are the spirit
In my step, dance, and praise.
You took my brokenness
And made me whole,
When I would have quit
You gave me love to live.

Pursuit

O child below
I run after you.

You are My heart's desire.
You are the one
For whom My heart burns.
You are the reason
I came to you.

I give you ears to hear
And eyes to see
Hands to comfort
The weary and wandering
So you can imitate Me.

Come to me
Don't run away.
I love you with great compassion.
Take My yoke
And be set free.

Free to run
To run with Me.

Questions

Some say they know You,
But I wonder if they do
    When they gaze up at the painted sky
    And only see shades and hue
Totally forgetting You.

Why do we grow up fatherless
    When You dwell so near?
How do we grow so deaf
    When You've given us ears to hear?
How do we have eyes that never see
    The wonders of Your mysteries?
And minds that reject You
    When it's You that gives us choice?
Why do we turn away
    From the grace bought at Your expense?
Is the lust of the flesh so satisfying
    That it dulls our need of You?
How do we live in the world You created
    And reject its origin?
When will the scales fall from our eyes
    As a waterfall
    And crash liked an ocean wave
    Answering the shore's call
    To take it away?
When will we see beyond limited natural sight
    Into the world You know and delight?
When will we hear Your voice
    Calling us to our real home?
Why and when?
    Just some of the many questions
We won't know until then.

Radiance

The sun of the universe shines
But it can't over power
The glory of Father, Son, and Holy Ghost
Creator of everything.
O Earth arise
And worship the glorious One.

Rain

Fall on us like rain.
Soften the soil of our hearts.
Bring life to our soul.
May our roots seek
depth only in You.
With Your warmth and life in us,
Make us like the farmer's field
Reaching to Your light above,
Maturing to bring a harvest
Glorious to You.

Fall on us like rain
So love defeats the hate
Until the blind see again
Deaf ears hear
'Til all the captives are set free
And the mute sing loud Your praise
Until those that mourn and grieve
Know the comfort of Your grace.

And when we have received....
Send us out like rain
Over the fields of grain
Taking warmth and water
To the growing harvest,
All for the Glory of Your Name.

Reflections and Reality

Thinking back on life
Pieces misplaced
Creeping up from behind
To this present place.

Hopes and dreams vanishing each day
All once hoped for – swiftly swept away
Erred ways of thinking
Apparent now
Inflicting pain
With tears dripping down.

As gloom completes for control
Pray for strength
From God's endless mercy and grace
Even if you feel you're withering by the hour.

Attacks and torments from within
From proud and unrepentant sin
As serenity flees
Cry for release.

Hurting and afraid wondering
If this temptation will ever cease?
The Lord will hold you tight in love
So you'll not fall prey to the enemy's sword.

He instills the hope in Tribulation's hour
He delivers and raises in His power
Uniting weak souls with saints above
Earth and Heavenly hosts singing His love.

In faith I ask for His will to be done
In the Name of the Father, Holy Ghost, and Son
In full unity as if and until
Heaven and Earth be One.

Rejoice

Rejoice, rejoice O holy children
Sing to Your God on high
For He has heard your prayers and supplications
And longs to dry the tears from your eyes.

Rejoice, rejoice O Jew and Gentile
Before the throne we all are one
Intercede now for one another
And for God's Kingdom to come.

Rejuvenation

Make my flesh
Your tablet of stone
Not written on with ink
But with the Holy Spirit of God.
Make me Yours
Convert these dry bones
Make them rise again
To praise and dance
Singing Shalom.

Remember Me

Our God wants to be remembered.
Hear His glory thunder as He makes Himself known.
In dreams and visions
He speaks to our spirit through His own.
The evidence of comfort,
Gentleness and loving-kindness.

Our God is the King of Glory.
Declarer of new things;
The answer to our prayers,
Brightness overcoming darkness and sin.
In days of Old,
The Ark of the Covenant
Evidence of communion.
In days since,
The Word as Flesh
Who dwelt among us.

Our God knows no evil
But stretches out His hand
To fallen man
And bring us His righteousness
Through Christ our Lord;
Sent to be known
Face to face:
Our refiner and redeemer;
Our healing grace.

Fear God and live,
With reverence,
Seek His face.
He is the fullness we desire,
The keeper of our soul,
The bringer of higher order,
The very love
Our heart yearns for.

Revelation

Against Thee and Thee only
have I sinned
and done this evil
in Thy sight.
Since my sin is against Thee
before Thee, I stand in repentance.
From Thee I seek wisdom
and bow in obedience.
Almighty and Most High God,
Creator of Heaven and earth,
I acknowledge my sinful ways:
my pursuit of worldly possessions,
enlightenment and intellect,
desiring power to persuade,
and with aspirations to be esteemed by man.
At Your altar, O God,
I surrender selfish desires,
stubbornness,
rebelliousness,
independence,
and my hardened heart.
I confess my failure to read Thy Word,
Pray in accord with Your Holy Spirit,
And continually seek Thy ways.

I have neglected to listen to Your voice,
fix my eyes steadfastly upon Your face,
to see the needs of my neighbors,
to live a Godly life,
and be an example in this world.

I confess to You, Sovereign King
        that my sinful ways are rooted in pride, lust,
        self-preservation and insecurity from the evil one
        or in temptations
        springing forth from seeds of human carnality.

In failing to heed Thy Word,
        I have nourished the desires of my flesh
                with its insatiable hunger.
        While my spirit starved,
                my bones protruded.
Malnourished, my vulnerability to temptation increased…
        And in my weakness, I succumbed to sin.
        As a leper, I turned away from the Beloved
                And cried, "Unclean, Unclean…Unworthy am I!"
        Outcast and alone in the darkness,
        Along the path of indifference, self-pity, laughter and folly,
                I turned from those seeking to heal
                my diseases and transgressions
and rejected Your loving grace, forgiveness,
and protection.
After such ignorance and folly
        My soul continued to want.
                I had eaten and was not satisfied,
                drank, and my thirst not quenched.
                I relaxed and enjoyed the spirits deception,
                but had not peace from Thee within.
In deficiency, I opened Thy Word,
        yet was cursed with guilt and condemnation.
As Thy Word blurred before my eyes,
        I beheld my sin,
        saw the evil one's grin
        and cried out in sorrow and great fear,
        "My God, what have I done?"

I perceived the severity of my transgressions
   and bowed humbly for my confession:
   "Against Thee and Thee only have I sinned
   and done this evil in Thy sight."
Even in my filth and unrighteousness
   Thy Word began to flow from my lips
   And I remembered the days when I feasted
   At Thy table, an undeserving, yet honored guest.
And in my spirit, I experienced both Glory and Evil
   Wrestling for my soul.

Then I heard the voice of my Lord say,
   "Rest and clear thy mind
   The evil one desires My Word to condemn you
   while you are unable to discern the voices."
Then I heard the demon proclaim,
   "Read now the truth of judgment
   in the Word of God! You have profaned
   His Holy Name!"
Shaken I rested, fully aware I had already been deceived.
When my mind cleared with the morning light
   I again sought truth at the throne of the Lord
   And bowed humbly at His feet of mercy and grace.
With shaken faith and broken heart,
   I surrendered to my loving God
And I heard the voice of the Beloved say,
   "Hear now and understand My words
   and your journey shall be steadfast on the path
   that leads to eternal joy…though there be trials along the way
   Lo I am with thee always."

"My child, there is permissiveness
   in the laws of man
   such that allow actions and attitudes
   contrary to the teachings of My Holy Word.

Little one, you have been born of My Spirit,
　　　you've been cleansed through and through,
　　　so there are ways of man, though lawful to him,
　　　are unholy to Me and unacceptable for you.
I require holiness, ownership, and authority
　　　your sin is not an earthly offense.
　　　It is one of pride, indifference, foolishness and disobedience.
Man will not condemn your actions
　　　for man pursues a wicked way
　　　estranged from me, led by the father of lies
　　　who seeks not My face.
I know your weaknesses as human flesh
　　　that your mind and heart are willing
　　　yet your flesh so weak.
　　　　　　I know, for I am Creator of all
　　　　　　Even of the dust of thee.
But you must understand precious child,
　　　Hearken forth your ear:
　　　　　　Your choices today shall pave the way
　　　　　　henceforth from your journey here.
　　　　　　If you seek the way of the ruler of the earth
　　　　　　　　living casually towards Me;
　　　　　　you live in danger of straying away
　　　　　　　　from the grace of the Prince of Peace.
　　　　　　For each and every action My child
　　　　　　Is either towards Me or away.

Yes, you have erred My child,
　　　but do not turn away in shame;
　　　Turn again unto Me now,
　　　While your ears know My name YAHWEH.
Heed the voice of the Lord Your God
　　　let not the tempter persuade you further into his abyss.
Renounce his power and his name where you stand
　　　in the Name of Jesus the Lord
and fix your eyes once again and march towards
The Eternal Promised Land.

Do not rely on your own strength
     Only I am able to deliver you.
     I tell you the truth
     It is evil that says that I will punish you.
     It is Satan who says you are condemned
     And have forfeited your peace forever,
     That your sins are unforgivable
     That you're eternally imprisoned by your sin.
Only I tell you the truth
     for Satan is the father of all lies.
Who is he to say whom I will forgive
     Was it he who was crucified?
Do not hearken a moment to his deception
     lest you fall into guilt and his pit of damnation
     where eternal fire awaits those who rejected
     the grace of the God Most High.

Hearken your ears unto My words
     and turn from your wicked ways
Seek again My Holy face
     with open heart and mind
     that I may once again fill you My child
     with My wisdom and peace
     and empower you with My overcoming strength,"
Thus saith the Lord God Almighty
Who Was, and Is, and Is to come.
Even so, come quickly Lord Jesus.

Rhema Faith

Glorious God
Revealed, yet unknown
I raise my voice
To Thee alone.
None other is worthy
Of honor or praise
Than You, Mighty Creator
Ancient of Days.

All Heaven and Earth
Will one day bow
But as for me
I do so now.
Praise and honor
For You, I desire;
In the world but not of it
For Your ways are higher.

Lead me to worship
In spirit and truth
To simply believe
Your Word is true
To understand, proclaim
And DO
So with all of my being
I live in one accord
With YOU.

River Currents

Meditations:
Job 28:10; Isaiah 66:12-13; John 7:38; Revelation 22:1-2

Currents flowing
observe it
study it
feel it
sit in it
enter it
join it
it's flowing
waiting...

Listen to instruction
prepare your mind
body and soul
come expecting
wait
trust
listen
patience
practice
skills develop
move farther
next step
come higher
excitement
dreams
experience
launch
balance
straight
turn
lean in
perfect the skills
feel the confidence
boldness...

Practice with faith
move with it
take authority
press onward
expecting more…

Read the currents
flowing
swift
calm
eddy
moving
unity
becoming one
one with the water
the vessel an extension
of yourself
currents swift
demanding
maneuvering
heeding the words of instruction
roll
ferry
turn in
and
w—a—i—t
w—a—i—t
w—a—i—t
NOW ACT!!
steady
full stroke
GO
no hesitation
draw
hook

hard
lean into it
lean in
not away
face it…
Press in
grasp it
fear not
roll
or escape
free
focus on the plan
concentrate
calm
execute
sequence
complete
freed…

Gather the scattered
signal
tow in
prepare
regroup
think it through
relive
evaluate
seek advice
make a plan
execute
try again
learn
face it
do it
again
and again
and again

until you overcome
Then
overcome
again…

Master it
proceed
tackle the next obstacle
and the next
grow in faith
and skill
apply
the experience

Skills enhanced by
challenges
new feats
apparently impossible
enveloped in waves
circling
mastering
enduring
facing fears
one after another
all our days
Bringing yet higher
more challenging
waves
falls
obstacles
crashing overhead
Triumph!

Unknowns
I respect you
Yet
I am not afraid
continuing through eternal days
bringing yet higher
more challenging
waves...

My instructor
My guide
Leads the way
Demonstrating
Teaching
Leading
Waiting
Celebrating
The passage.

River of Life

O River, I hear you whispering my name
Drawing me closer so I'll never be the same.
Wash over me
Wash over me
Hold me in Your embrace.
Wash over me
Wash over me
Lord, I long to see Your face.

River of life, spring of my days
Cleanse me and make me whole.
Listen…
Can you hear it trickling down?
There's a river growing with a mighty flow
Raging down from His throne.
A river of love and healing,
A long flowing white river
Like the train of a wedding gown.

I hear the river calling
"Come and be cleansed
Come into the waterfall
And rest in the mist.
Close your eyes
Laying distractions aside
Dive in deep
Leave the world behind."

Wash over me River of Life.
Wash over me 'til all carnality dies.
Wash over me, Wash over me,
Wash me clean, Spirit of life.

River of life,
Spirit of life,
Make me one with You.
O make me one –with YOU!

Run Until I Fly

Lord I wanna run – until I fly.
I wanna worship You
And cast all else aside.
Rip away all that constrains me,
Steer fear and distraction away.

I wanna run – until I fly.
Break off the chains of this life
That keep me from You..
I wanna soar – 'til I see You face to face.
I wanna run until I fly,
Right into Your embrace.

Because there's nothing
Greater than You;
No greater goodness,
Nothing more true.
I wanna run – until I fly,
Cause without You
I'm not satisfied.

Sacrificial Lamb

The dying Lamb
Bleeds all alone
On the cross
For which He was born.
Heaven and Hell remembered
Become the doors
To resurrect life
And defeat the foe.
Knowing the outcome
His soul cries out,
"Father forgive them!"
"It is finished."
The sky turns dark
And the earth quakes,
The Temple veil torn
From the top they say.
His life of love halted,
Surely a mistake,
For He promised a Kingdom
Before the end of His days.

Is this God's wrath
Or salvation's sweet song?
Why does it seem so
That the enemy won?
Death glares at my Savior's soul.
Evil lurks with hate in his eyes.
Yet my Beloved storms the gates of Hell
And frees the captives with His keys and a shout.
Though dead on that cross,
Jesus is alive.
Satan must flee,
Jesus reigns on high.
Hear the news, ye men of earth,
Heaven shouts Victory!

Satan is defeated.
Death to the enemy's curse.
Hear the news, ye men of Earth,
The Lord shouts Victory!
The battle is won.
Salvation's hope is offered for everyone!
He rose again and ascended to Heaven
To prepare you a place
And He shall come again
Just as He promised on that day.

Seasons

Too soon the birth of spring
Transforms to scorching summer days.
Greens fade to brown and thirst for rain,
As daylight slowly fades
And midnight brings its kiss of frost
With autumn's burst of color
And leaves releasing their hold on life
Dancing away with cooler breezes,
Leaving their former home naked and bare
Their previous days of glory
Only a memory now.

Then comes winter's blustery frigid biting
And in this life of death
The virgin snow blankets the earth in beauty
Preserving her for spring.
Yet, seldom does it seem too soon
That the hope of spring draws near,
But without fail by God's design
Winter's snowy blankets melt
And cold rains turn warm again,
Buds spring forth and prevail
Life beating death on earth again.

As it goes with changing seasons
Life rotates on its own axis
And if we will but learn from trees
That our hope of glory is both now
And in days to come,
We shall be encouraged to remain
Rooted and grounded to endure passing seasons.
Break not O mighty maple or oak
Though pressed and blown by wicked winds.
Your life is within and will spring forth again.

Secret Places

I wish to go
To the darkest rooms of your soul
To bring them light.
I wish to penetrate
Your weakest points
And bring them strength.
I wish to go
To your greatest fear
And conquer it with faith.

I wish to go
To your broken heart
And massage it with My redeeming grace.
I wish to make the journey
Past the image of pretense
       The crust you construct
        To protect your ego
Through the plains
Over rolling hills
Across treacherous mountains
Beyond scorching valleys
Farther than the deserts and jungles terrain
Deeper than the bottom of the ocean
Into your soul's molten flame
Where you are
And there is no other
The only fingerprint of you
For there I will find your truth
And it is there
We
       Can
           Linger
               Forever…
Knit in God's amazing grace.

Selah

I've been so sure
    For some time now
That this is where I'd stay
But recently the Lord has said
    It's time I move
    And I must be on my way.
I'm not sure where or when
    This is to come about
But I've a knowing that is so strong
    It cancels any and all doubt.

Father show me and guide me
I'm yielded to Your way
I have so many questions and thoughts
    Without the words to express
    The meanings to convey
But the greatest desire in my heart
    Is to do Your will
Jesus take my hands and guide my feet
    Calm my mind and heart
    With "peace be still."

Thank You, O Lord God
    For revelation of Your will
I need Your strength and courage
I know it's Your voice I hear whispering
    "Trust Me, for lo,
    I'm with you still."
Father show me
    And guide me across the rising seas.
Assure me in this confusion
    Only You are the breath I breathe.

Lord Jesus, I see You
        As if You're walking on the sea.
I hear You calling as You did Your disciples in Galilee
"It is I, don't be afraid!"

I see Your eyes and outstretched arms
        I know You bid me to "come."
Focus my eyes on You alone
        You know my frame is weak and frail.
Of my own strength, I will surely fail
        But I know by faith, You, O Lord,
        Always prevail.
Quiet all within me
        That doesn't trust or understand.
I kneel at Your feet, O God
        My life is in Your hands.
I see and feel Your anointing oil
        Flowing from my head to my feet,
        Soak me – rub it in – consecrate me.
Change all I've ever been
        That dishonored You
Thy Kingdom come and now Thy will be done
        On Earth as it is in Heaven.

You are a shield
        Around me Lord.
You bestow glory
        On Your own.
You lift my head
        And crown me
        As an heir to Your throne.
To You I cry aloud
        And You answer from Your Holy hill.
I will lie and sleep to rise again
        Until Your work for me is done.

Servant's Prayer

Lord I long to see Your face
In this dry and thirsty land
Yet, it seems I'm so easily drawn away
Help me overcome and understand.

I want to know You like I know myself
Unveiled with no mist or walls between
No pretense, no hiding
Naked yet unashamed.

I seek Your glory as my covering
Worldly wisdom and pursuits forsaken
As a bride on her wedding day
Nothing in my sight but You!

Too often I'm so distracted here
By the daily obligations of this life
I struggle so often
With how to manage my time.

I want it to be You I hear
Not all this other interference
I know You've been here and are here now
But my heart longs for a more intimate closeness.

Draw me closer to Your Holy Throne
'Til I am no more
I long for Your presence O Lord
I desire Your glory as my breath!

I want to seek nothing more than You alone
Your presence burning in me
Nothing but Your will and way
Your Kingdom done through me, I pray.

Servitude

I hear Your voice calling me
To places I've never been.
I know You want me to pray
For those I've never met.
And by Your grace and mercy
I will boldly speak
Of Your greatness and splendor
And how You set me free.

Come now Holy Spirit
Descend upon us here.
Rise up in us Your people
So we lovingly run Your race.
We don't have all the answers,
So to You we cry
And You hear us and reply
Rise up, O spring of joy.

I run to You
I run to You
I run to You again.
Nothing can separate us
Not even my failures and sin.
I run to You
I run to You
I run to You again.
My heart longs for You
Draw me closer in.
O my heart longs for You
I'm here for You to send.

Shaken

Jesus, I've lived
Like my life was my own.
I've saved and stored
Up for myself in barns;
Then Your fire
Descended on my soul.
So I yield, I yield
I can't stand it any more.

Breathe into me
Your life from above.
I exchange all I have
For all You want from me.
Bring Your Heaven
On earth through me.
I yield, I yield
More of You is all I need.

Spectrums of light flow
Deeply in my veins.
I'm amazed at the love I feel
And I've no loss only gain.
I empty my barns
So I've more room for You.
I yield, I yield
Consume me with Your flame.

Your seed in me is fire,
Burning bush in my soul.
More than flesh can stand
It's Holy ground, I know.
Hold me in Your presence
Purify my soul
To yield, to yield
Living sacrifice of love.

Shallow Waters
{Friendship}

I swim in shallow water
>because shallow water is safe.
>I can see how deep it goes,
>I can see what might be hiding below,
>I can see the power of the current's flow.

I play there safely, often without support,
>No vicious waves or tide there
>to knock me down in sport;

Just a gentle unthreatening diversion,
>like shade in summer heat;

A frivolous exchange in shallow water,
>lightly splashing my feet.

Deep water dismays me
>the depth I cannot see
>and in those depths
>I do not know
>what may be lurking
>that could harm me.

I know I can swim
>but am I strong enough
>to stay afloat out there
>when crashing waves rise
>and knock me under
>before I catch my breath?

Survival requires skill and strength
>And the tide's ebb and flow
>Is so far beyond my control,
>That the deep water is a place
>I just cannot go.

But if you like the deeper water
>I'll go with you and watch you play
>And I'll stay in the shallows
>Where I know I'm safe.

Sing

Sing O sing
Body, soul and spirit
Praise the Lord
For His mighty love.
Sing O sing
Body, soul, and spirit
For you are redeemed
By the blood.
Exalt the Lord
Rejoice
Magnify.
Exalt the Lord
Rejoice
Magnify!

Sing Honor and Praise

Sing honor and praise unto His Name
Give with cheerful heart and proclaim
Walk in brotherly love and sustain
The will of the Lord reigns.

Sing My Soul

Sing my Soul
Of heaven's beauty.
Sing O Spirit
Before His throne of grace.
O body draw
From His well of strength.

Reach up to His arms
For He's Abba.
Walk O feet
Righteous in His ways.
Dance in victory,
He's overcome the grave.

Meditate O mind
On His love enduring.
Beat O heart
A new song you sing.
Soar O spirit
Unto the heavens.

For His name is Yahweh
Yahweh
That once unspeakable Name.
Yahweh
Yahweh
The only one worthy
Of my praise.

Yahweh
Yahweh
Friend of my soul
Who was
Who is
Who is to come
Yahweh!

Sing O Sing

Sing O sing body, soul and spirit.
Sing O sing of His mighty power.
Sing O sing,
He's my refuge and high tower.
Sing O sing of His wondrous love.

Sing O sing body, soul and spirit.
Sing O sing of His healing grace.
Sing O sing,
Let us receive and not make haste.

Sing O sing body, soul and spirit.
Sing O sing of salvation's love.
Sing O sing,
For He's redeemed us by His blood.
Descend Holy Spirit like a dove.

Sing O sing body, soul and spirit.
Sing O sing to my All in All.
Sing O sing,
Break every dividing wall.

Sing O sing body, soul and spirit.
Sing O sing of His unity.
Sing O sing,
As the Trinity is one, so shall we be
Whether on earth or in the heavenlies.

Sing O sing body, soul and spirit.
Sing O sing no more death or sorrow.
Sing O Sing,
Life everlasting, love forevermore.

Sing O sing body, soul and spirit.
Sing O sing, He forsakes not His own.
Sing O sing,
Full of rejoicing
In Him, you are never alone.

Sing O sing body, soul and spirit.
Sing O sing to the Mighty King.
Sing O sing,
Hear O earth, the angels sing.

Sing O sing body, soul and spirit.
Sing O sing, Thy Kingdom come.
Sing O sing, with all creation
Thy will be done.

Sing O sing body, soul and spirit.
Sing O Heaven and Earth be glad.
Sing O sing,
Liberty in God's perfect Lamb.

Exalt, Rejoice, Magnify!
Exalt, Rejoice, Magnify!

Sitting in the Pouring Rain

Sitting in the pouring rain
I thought I heard the thunder
Clap Your name
And I wondered if it could be You.

Closed my eyes
Shut out the world
And sat still all night
Waiting…waiting for You.

Realized in the quietness
It had been too long
Since I'd let Your voice
Speak and calm the storm.

Forgive me Lord
For pushing You aside
Being too busy
To give You any time.

Dear Lord speak to me again
Through the rain and through the wind
Through the rocks
And beauty that surrounds.

Sitting in the pouring rain
I heard my Father say
"There are just a few things
I have to say."

"Turn now from your sin and shame.
Come to Me and obey.
The price for your sin is paid.
And I'm waiting to give you everything."

Sitting in the pouring rain
Thunder clapped and I heard Your name
Freeing me from all sin and shame
That's why I sit here, in the pouring rain.
Sitting in Your waterfall
Soak me through 'til I'm strong
Refresh me with Your breath of life
So I rise, to proclaim Salvation's Song.

You wash me clean
That's why I stay
On this solid rock today
Sitting in the pouring rain.

Why would I want to go away
When You are here
To cleanse my soul
And heal all my brokenness?

I come to this place to seek Your face
And sing praises to Your Holy Name:
My God, my provider, lover, and friend
My God, my very life within.

Slain

My soul is slain
Surrendered to God
Covered I cling
To Christ's atoning blood.
I now breathe
In rest and peace,
Though I have so many questions
With answers I don't know
It doesn't change where I am
Or where I plan to go.

Repent and let the offense go
I hear it well and I know
Yet, the scandalon
Tempts me so,
And I'm held in a snare,
Death's laughing stare
Oh Lord, help me let go.

I set my life aside.
Like a crown, I lay it down,
Including my pride,
Just to be found
Faithful in You.

God forgive
My lack of faith;
For not believing enough
That You've already delivered me
From this place.
Forgive me again,
I want to believe
Yet my flesh cringes afraid.

Father of life
Father of love
Strengthen my spirit to rule.
Assure me I'm safe in Your bosom.
When all I've known
Blows away with the wind,
Hide me under Your wings
Until I'm strong and keen.
Breathe Your life into my soul
Cleanse my lips with Your coals.

Manifest Your work in me;
Slay my flesh
So my spirit soars,
Higher and higher
Than ever before
No fear
Forsaking all
Until we are joined as One.

Lord hold me
Let me not stray.
I pray faith and hope
For the downcast brow
For each moment
As I live in You,
My God that ever lives
cannot die.
May I live
Full of love
Praising You
With dance and song
All my days.

Peace in freedom
And liberty,
Build me Lord
Precept upon precept.
Establish Your truth
In my every step.
I want to trust You more
Teach me to obey
And be more like Jesus
Than I am today.

Calm my mind
Dry each tear.
Dispel each and every fear.
I long to soar
With angels on high
Drawing nigh
Round your throne in awe.
So I set my life aside;
Like a crown, I lay it down,
Including my pride.
Just to be found
Faithful in You.

Slopes of Grief

I don't understand why people lie
I heard you say "call anytime"
Yet when I do, it sounds as though I bother you.
How do you expect me to call again
When I do and you tell me to just go to bed?

I ache with pain,
Sorrow overwhelms
And when I call in the darkness of grief's depths
I'm sorry I bothered you in your secure little nest.
And I get the little spiel on grief that comes and goes
Like that isn't something I already know.

I've blundered around three days now
Unable to focus, hear, or figure out
Where I go from here.
And then the rejection today
To be totally ignored like plague.
And this is the justice I fought for
And that our young men and women die?

I wasn't prepared for this hurt and pain
I thought I was on the road to living again
When on the thin ice with a split and crack
I plunge back into the icy waters
That threatened not to give me back.
God why are people so cold and cruel
To mourn the dead and ignore the living?
To trivialize pain like a headache
That will be gone in the morning?

Rachel cries out still for the death of her babes
And still no comfort soothes her soul
For they are dead and gone once for all.
All the dreams unfulfilled.

Where there was love and youthful laughter
Now only silence that screams even louder
A void no amount of sleep will ever cure
A hole only God can cleanse and make pure.
So don't be surprised next week when I don't come by
And the message is I won't be
Since it's a waste of our time.
Being normal and all, like you said
There's nothing else to say or do.
I played by the book and got smashed with its slam
I'm tired of the pain and people shams.

So I'm spending my time with God
The only one I've known
Who's never said or acted like He didn't have time;
The only one who answers and comforts me when I call.
The only one who knows how I grieve in the lies
And cry alone, silently in the shadows of night.
The only one who knows how to comfort my soul
When all I want to do is end all these painful feelings
and lies
When I'm told to go to bed
And tomorrow will be better
When you're no better a predictor of that
  Than the weather.

Good-bye now and I'm sorry I called.
I won't call again – even if it means I stay here stalled.
I'll freeze to death before I ask again
While all the time wondering - Why people say
"Call anytime."
When they don't really mean it anyway.
I hope no one else calls you tonight
without hope and ready do die;
Because sleep is deceptive
when suicide sings her song "Ending Misery."

Forgive me please if I sound so cruel
I called once again
And made myself the fool.
The pain is just too much to bear alone
But it's obvious now
There's no other road to go.
Sleep well, you say - so at least one of us will.
And thank you for helping the best you could
In a time just a bit too surreal
Beyond that with which I know how to deal.

So alone here I sit.
Freezing under blankets and my head with heat
wrapped.
I pray I need not reside here long –
I don't trust my confidence is that strong.
There's nothing else much to say
Than I hope you never have to face
Rejection's pain
In the eyes of those you see again and again
Whether in reality or in rumination.

Song of Adoration

Holy— Holy—Holy
Glory be to God on High
And praise to Him here on earth
Redeeming God – Alive.

Sing praises, sing praises, O Israel.
Your redeemer will soon come again
Restoring those who have sought His heart
And then take the whole body home.

Our Father, Who art in Heaven
Hallowed be Thy Name
Thy Kingdom come Thy will be done
On Earth as it is in Heaven.

Glory be to God on High
Maker of Heaven and Earth
Redeeming Savior, Lord of Grace
Of whom I belong.

Praise the Father, O praise the Son
Praise the Holy Spirit, too,
The three in one, blessed union
My life, my hope, my all.

I have no other need than You
For You supply my every need.
I only ask and seek Your will
And You give more than I can receive.

Open my eyes Lord and my ears
Until I see You everywhere I go.
Fill me with Your love and peace,
Power and compassion to soften hearts of stone.

Song of the Redeemed

This world we live in
Is a dry and thirsty land
But we – God's children
Can go to our Father
And drink from the cup in His hand.

Promises of provision
Await the redeemed.
Hallelujah, hallelujah
We give glory to Your Name.
Hallelujah, hallelujah
Let our praises be
A sweet smelling incense
At Your throne.

Salvation and healing
Jehovah Jireh, my Sozo;
These are our bread and wine
His stripes and blood.
With healing and salvation
I shout in liberty!

I will pick up the tools
My God gives to me
To battle and defeat
Even my greatest enemy.

The weapons of my warfare
Not of flesh and blood
But mighty to the pulling down
Of every stronghold.

He provides
He is my strength
He is all I need
He is Alpha and Omega
I am nothing
But victorious in Him.

He's my God
To Him, my voice I raise
No other is worthy
Of the victory shouts of praise!

Soul Cry

Father, I come to You broken and weak
My arms trembling and knees feeble
I wobble standing
I'm unable to hold myself up.
My tongue stammers as I try to speak
And my thoughts spiral out of control
        If I have any at all.
Feelings anchor me motionless
        And prevent me from escape
Everything in my soul says
        IF I was really strong
        I would be able to endure
Yet You say in weakness I am strong.

My soul and spirit struggle against one another
To take charge over my thoughts and ways
And I'm left with daunting thoughts and visions
        Of being rent in two.
I struggle with my humanity, Lord
Insecurities, frailties, distractions
        And vulnerability to sin against You.

YOU, my Wonderful Creator, Redeemer,
        Savior, Peace,
        Helper, Guide, Light,
        Perfect Love,
        and unending Father.
Father of Glory, The Eternal One.

Forgive me for struggling against You
For lacking faith in You, in Your ability,
        Your willingness and Your power
But mostly for lacking in my belief of Your love.

Forgive me for fearing You
For fearing I will never measure up
For fearing my failure to hear You

For fearing the rejection of men
  More than embracing You.
Forgive me for fearing loneliness
  And not seeing You in that place.
Forgive me for not receiving the compassion
  Your Holy Spirit offers my weary soul.
I admit my inadequacy in this flesh of dust
My own blood and sweat pours from my flesh
  in the form of works
And I wonder why I am anemic and faint.
I want to do so much
And struggle with the defeat of time, resources and
knowledge
  Of how to achieve these goals.

I hear the world cry "Live and let live!"
  "I did it my way" and "You only live once."
My heart wails as I attempt to walk a path
  Worthy of Your calling
  Amidst worldly ways.
Forgive me for finding the darkness of this world
  and its persistent sins of self-indulgence
  so appealing.
I confess this to You, Father
Because at the end of my life
I long for my heart to present You with a sanctified
offering
  Refined with fire
  Worthy of Your praise.
You've given me so much – actually everything
And when I meet You face to face
My spirit longs to present You with increased souls.
The only worthy return of the investment
You have entrusted to me.
Lord guide me so I don't stand empty handed
With no interest for You on that day.

Teach me to be a good and faithful servant.
This task only You can do.
Philosophy tears me between tolerance and division
Psychology sways me toward the beliefs of men
Science tempts me to worship knowledge
Music both worships and denies You
Economy encourages me to save up treasures for myself
Government entices the lust for power
And religion without You is feigning folly.
In the midst of all this infertile ground
My soul longs for You.

And though man never asked
For You to come to him in his weakness
And expected a different portrayal of Messiah,
You came.
You met the prophets of Old where they were:
            In a burning bush and belly of a fish
            In blood sacrifices
And the Ark of the Covenant
            In tents and temples
            In rivers and wombs
            On the water and on the mount
You were there for them
And are still there for us.
We cannot escape Your goodness
            Or Your wrath.

Prepare the hearts of those who love You
With an unfeigning, unending, passionate, lavishing
love.
That same love You showed usward
In Jesus, Your Son.
Create in us a clean heart
Renew the right spirit in Your people.
Purify our hearts O Lord
Teach us to pray and hear You again.
Teach us to love and receive love
From You and Your children
'Til You come.
Shalom and Amen.

Soul Searching

Lord, I've examined my heart
And found fault within
In attitudes and thoughts.
I've spoken when silence was needed
And remained silent when boldness was required.
I've said "Nice to see you"
When I really didn't care.
I've murmured, gossiped and complained
Instead of showing love and faith.
I've wanted for my own pleasure
Refusing to share.
I've cared more about what others would think
Than yielding my will to Yours…
Cared how I looked before men
Than how You saw my sin.
Cared more of what man believed
Than how Your heart I must have grieved.
I've used excuses and cried out "Grace, grace."
When I should have repented
And fallen on my face.
My flesh tempts me so
And cries loudly to be heard
And in weakness, I don't try
Quickly giving in;
Swinging open wide
The gate for sin.

Teach me
And change me, O God.
Father, this I pray
Lest your judgment consume me
And in me find - No good thing.
Reign in me Spirit of God
I yield my heart to You
To be found worthy by Your indwelling
Faithful to You
Now and at the end of my days.

<u>Speak</u>

Speak to me Holy Spirit
My form of dust requires Your sustenance.
When my strength is fading,
Teach me to seek counsel in Your Word
So that Your Spirit will resuscitate my dying flesh
And seal breaches in my earthen vessel.
Imprint Your precepts on my heart.
Sustain me with Your power and peace.
Speak to me Holy God.
Fill my empty vessel to overflowing
With Your wisdom and love.
Grant me the ears and lips of Your prophets of Old
To proclaim your message of salvation and purity
So that the words of your servant,
Actions of my flesh
And meditations of my heart
Will be acceptable to You.
O Lord – My Strength and my Redeemer,
Speak to me O Holy One of Israel.
Your words are life
Your words – my sacrifice and praise
Your Holy Word my only hope
From deceitful wicked ways.
Let Your words flow through me
As life-giving blood
Through unobstructed veins
That those near and far from Your heart
Hear Your hope and truth
And return from deceived ways.

Brother listen now carefully
Do you know what Satan
wants from you?
Our fight is not against flesh and blood
But the fruit of Galatians 5:22.

Speak to Me Holy Spirit

Speak to me Holy Spirit
Your servant needs words to say
To the downcast and unlovable
I meet along life's way.

I need to hear what You would say
If You were here right now.
I need the love and compassion
You demonstrated and spoke about.

Burn Your desires
Deep within my heart
To meet the needs of others
That the world doesn't have time for.

I long to demonstrate Your love
And amazing grace
Your power to heal
And resurrect the dead from the grave.

Speak to me Holy Spirit
Speak clearly so I can hear
What to say to those who need You
Before they pass me by.

Spirit Led

If you want to know
what God wants you to do,
just ask Him.
He gladly gives His wisdom
and His guidance
to those who request.
He protects the righteous,
He guides the humble
And teaches them His way.

Just as you trusted Jesus to save you
just trust Him
and obey.
He's more powerful
than any problem
trying you today.
Do not be anxious about tomorrow
Let today be sufficient for today.

The Lord will fulfill
His purpose for you,
His love endures forevermore.
Oh children hear Him
for we are mirrors that brightly reflect
the glory of our King
And as the Spirit of the Lord works within us
We become more like Him.

Listen to the Lord
as He answers
the prayers of His faithful
"I no longer call you slaves
From now on
I call you friends.
Yes, even joint heirs with Jesus,"
declares the Almighty.

Spirit Prayer

In Your presence
With music praising
The Spirit led my downcast soul in sobbing
to the Lord.
Show Your faithfulness again,
for this vessel of flesh
draw Your sword.
Shine O Mighty God
Through the despairing darkness.
Hover over me with Your peace.
Silence the lies and distortions of truth.
Cease their stealing hopes and dreams,
End the plagues against Your redeemed.
O God, Creator of breath, width and height
Speak again creative light.
As You spoke in the beginning.
Separate our day from night
And call it good in Your sight.

Breathe Your life
Into these nostrils of dust.
Revive our minds
With Your comforting hush.
Through me, Holy Spirit
Guide this vessel
Safely through this night
To behold again
Your morning light.
Holy Spirit
Very life of life
Quiet the soul
Longing to feel Your touch,
Giving drink from your well
'Til they are satisfied.

Revive us again
spirit, body, and soul
Until we are whole.

Bring remembrance of all
That is Spirit and Truth
So our worship
Is pleasing to You.
Fill us with Your power,
Confidence and willingness to obey
That Jesus showed us
When He walked upon this earth.
For now Your temple
Reigns in us.
Let there be nothing we cannot do
Because of our obedience to You.

This I ask in intercession
For our temporal house,
Our living sacrifice
Lifted up to You to edify.
For I know the thoughts
You have toward man
Of peace, not evil
For a future and hope
For us to seek You
With all our heart.

Then the angel spoke
Softly in my ear,
"O man of dust, do not fear
Jehovah Shammah, He is here."

Stand Fast My People

"Listen again and heed My instruction
Stand fast – yes, stand fast.
The earth will shake beneath you
and try to swallow you up.
The winds both fiery hot
and blustery cold
will blow against you
and slap your face.
The tormented waves of the sea
will try to flood your soul
BUT YOU ARE MY PEOPLE
AND WILL NOT BE SNATCHED OUT OF MY HAND.

So when the ground beneath you trembles,
nations wage war against one another
and the heavens whirl in fury
cutting a path of destruction –
REMEMBER THAT YOU ARE MINE
WORSHIP ME – TRUST ME – LISTEN ONLY TO ME
IN ALL THINGS
BE STILL AND KNOW
THAT I AM GOD.
Take shelter under the refuge of My wings
for I am the creator of the heavens and the earth.
In all confusion,
My people rest.
I AND I ALONE AM LIFE TO YOUR BONES
I AM YOUR ETERNAL GLORY.
Cease from your labors and be still,
For the Victory is Mine,"
saith the Lord.

Stir the Waters

Stir the stagnant waters of my soul.
Pour in Your love and make me whole.
I seek no longer, traditions of men,
But lay my crowns down at your feet again.
O stir the stagnant waters of my soul.
There's no other who can restore my love.
Stir within me a greater desire for Your ways
So I can flow with You
In Your amazing grace.

Submission

Alpha and Omega
Beginning and End
Alef and Tov
Yes and Amen

You peered into my heart full of sin
And in Your grace and mercy forgave me even then.
Sift my wounds and decree
The dross be purified with fire.
Revive my walk with You
Pleasing to Your desire.

Alpha and Omega
Beginning and End
Alef and Tov
Yes and Amen!

Surrender

I surrender
In the pinions of Your wings
White down feathers
Fluttering.
Children resting on Your breast
Safe from harm, torment and death.
The King of Glory
My shelter and rest
Penetrating warmth
Eternal love
As far as East is from West
All Your promises
Amen and Yes.

Abba Father
I proclaim
I am a Royal Child,
A welcomed wedding feast guest.
In love and adoration
We Your children sing praise:
Glory to our God
And to Jesus our King

Elders circling Your throne
Endlessly in Heaven,
While we of the earth
Hide in the pinions of Your wings
Seeking Your holiness.
We feel Your heart beat
As we cling to
White down feathers fluttering.

More wise than a serpent
More gentle than dove or lamb
The King of Glory protects
His chicks with outstretched hand.
Every tribe and tongue
Following the Lamb
To the refuge
Of God's own land.

Open up ye gates
Let the King of Glory come in.
With white down fluttering
Heaven resounds.
And in those feathers fluttering
Those once lost now are found.
All the strength and love we need
In Him are found.
He lacks nothing
And offers His children everything,
If we will rest under
White down fluttering wings.

Whatever joy or challenge
This life may or may not bring,
I offer it at His feet.
No other grace than His for me.
The only God that came to man as babe,
The only one that came to suffer and die,
To draw all man under His wingspan
But letting each one choose his own way.

When my life is someday over
May it be said I was faithfully found
Only seeking His Face
And will be found
Under the pinions of His wings
Close to His heart in the white down fluttering.

Tattoo of the Palms

My heart soars freely
as the eagle above
Full of my Father's blessings
granted with overflowing love.
There's no headwind of guilt
no wind shear of fear
No anchor snaring
insecurity or shame.

For I fly celestially
with Jesus as my guide.
My flight the Spirit's wedding gift
for His beloved bride.

I AM FREE
No longer bound
FREE in His love
Soaring Heaven bound!

My hands wave highly
in praise to my God.
Jehovah of Abraham
YAHWEH, the Great I AM.
The friend of the captive
in chains sorely bound,
Locksmith of the prison door
where once I was found.

My voice will praise
His Holy Name
The One above all others
Who made all things.
The Alpha and Omega
the One who does not change.
The Beginning and the End
Eternally – the same.

For I fly celestially
with Jesus as my guide.
My flight the Spirit's wedding gift
for His Beloved bride.

I AM FREE
No longer bound
FREE in His love
Soaring Heaven bound!

I raise my hands
and lift my voice.
I give my heart, my soul
and each choice,
To bless the One that
knows all things
And even so
loves me just the same.

Satan's words
I now shield
Because I know
only God can heal.
My Father is Love
and I am His own.
I know He loves me,
on His palms it shows.

Teach Me Lord

Teach me Lord
> How to pray with the passing of each day
> Show me where to turn when I am lost
> And bring me home safely in the light of Your way.

Teach me Lord
> How to live in such a way I can forgive
> Make me like virgin snow free of my sin
> For only then can my new life begin.

Teach me Lord
> How to love when I feel love has died
> To remember Your Son filled with compassion and love
> Direct me to the sunrise when the day is done.

Teach me Lord
> How to comfort each and every one
> Allow me to understand the old as well as the young
> Help me realize the importance of carrying out Your will.

Teach me Lord
> How to follow Thee and never lose sight of Your way
> Grant me boldness to be honest and share Your grace
> So we all may rejoice with glorious sound.

Teach me Lord
> How to serve being true to Your Word
> Be my strength when I can no longer fight
> And when the battle is over – stay with me through the night.

Teach me Lord
> How to teach when ears refuse to hear
> Let me know You are near when I am weary
> Bring to my remembrance that I am never alone.

Teach me Lord
> How to thank You for Your love and grace
> To include thanks in my prayers
> To show my gratitude and acknowledgement of Your care.

Dear Lord
      There is so much more guidance I need of You this day
      So much more wisdom and Your enduring grace
      I pray Thee to keep me teachable to Your way.
Teach me Lord
      All I should know to help others learn and grow
      Be with all who gather in Thy Holy Name
      And dearest Lord…Teach us all how to pray.

Thank You

Thank you Jesus
For this day.
Thank you
For Your warm embrace.
Thank you
For taking my place
On the cross,
For leading the way
To the Father
Who is no longer far away.
Thank you
For the Holy Spirit's reign
And for the power of Your Name.
Thank you Jesus
I'm no longer the same,
I've legs no longer lame
Because of the Holy Spirit's flame.
I thank you
On bended knee
For everything
You've done for me.
Thank you
That now I'm free
Living in perfect liberty,
For once blind eyes that now see,
For salvation,
For calming the seas of my life,
For Kingdom's keys,
And the new song in my heart.

Thank You Father

We thank you, Father
For Your Holy Word.
You bless us, Your people
And grant us the honor
To know Your heart.

We pray to You and we know
You hear our prayers
And dry each and every tear.
You are a Holy loving Father
And we love You.

We thank You Jesus
For leading us home.
You paid the price
To make us right
Before the Father on the throne.

Thank you Father
For Your Holy Spirit
Empowering us to do Your will.
Instill in us, today and forever
A greater desire to hear and obey.

O Father
Wash us now.
Cleanse our hearts and our minds.
Refresh us to rise
And honor Your Name.

The Aman Belay Trust
Explanation of Title

Aman -   [Strong's #539] is a Hebrew word. #540 is the Aramaic form of the same. It means – to confirm, support, stand firm, be enduring, to trust and believe. The word AMEN is derived from this word and means "sure, so be it." Aman is one of the very few words that translates into every language.

Belay – is a word of French origin that I learned while rappelling in the Appalachian Mountains. It means to be secured, fastened to one end of a rope. When you attach yourself to a rope anchored safely by another, this is a verbal announcement for that person to know you are relying on them for their support and safety.

Combined, I used the two words to acknowledge trust in God by anchoring oneself to Him, giving total trust and security to the Almighty, just as one rappelling does with their partner prior to stepping out in faith over the edge of the mountain.

The Aman Belay Trust

When life is blight and scattered in disarray
And the Nor'easters blow their bitter frozen rains
And hailstones fall pounding the ground
When the clouds descend for days on end
When the wind shear is no pilot's friend
When you're wedged in the crevasse
     Of pressure and gloom
When the advice of others is
     "Hold on tight, this too shall pass soon"
As your hands soaked in blood lose their grasp…
Hold only to your faith in God's Word
All else forego
Untangling your fears from the snares below.

For it's only in desisting sophistication
That man finds he resides in God's shadow
The Creator, Almighty, Unchanging
Everlasting in control!

When you fail in hope of yourself and others
In coldness of heart or heat that smothers
When in disgust, anger or ultimate dejection
Or paralysis of dire depression
Torment of confusion or oppression
Even in times of obsession with possessions
In regression, transgression, indiscretion
And especially in prayer, introspection and intercession
Seek not the answers in human intelligence and
sophistication
Cease the folly of man's self-guided spiritual
progression…
For there is no end of man's self-seeking perfection.

Entrust your care to the Lord of Creation
The Lord of Heaven and Incarnation
The One who experienced the transfiguration
Who knew men's heart without confession
The Sacrificial Lamb to Death and destruction
The Jesus of the tomb and the Resurrection
The ascender to Heaven awaiting return
The First, the Last, Unchanging and Everlasting.

Close your eyes
Feel the air
Watch the snowflake
     And raindrop, too.
Watch the lightning stretch
     And the hurricane brew.
Have you been where they're from?
Will you go where they'll go?
Yet do you doubt their reality
     Their beauty, fury, or awe?
Lord teach us to trust in You.

The Angels Wait

The angels wait in the Heavens today
For God's people to pray.
The angels wait in the Heavens today
For God's people to pray.

Lift up holy hands.
Sing with voices of praise.
Give with a cheerful heart.
Love in His Name.

The Father sits upon His throne,
The Son at His right hand.
The alms of His chosen ones
An honorable incense to Him.

Praise and honor Father and Son
And the Holy Ghost the same.
Empower angels to wield their swords
To enact the words the righteous pray.

As the incense rises
I see glory on every angel's face.
Swords drawn, wing span wide
Acting on behalf of men who praise the Lord,
According to the will of the Father.
In the Name of the Son,
Spoken by the saints
The righteous, chosen of God.

The Calling

Welcome to My fire
Burning hot and strong
Cleansing your mortal soul
Melting you away
Until all impurities are gone
Refining fire
Burn hotter than before
For all My children are of purest gold.
Don't run away
Come running to My fire
Come little one
Come home.

Welcome to My fire
Brightest white so Holy
Reflection of the Glory of His Highest
Holy Spirit, bring your searing coals
Touch my lips
And I shall be whole.
Come little ones
Come
Don't run away
Make me Your home.

Welcome to My fire
Eternal burning bush
Just as Moses saw
You are standing on Holy Ground
Listen to My voice
Heed My call
My heart burns for you.

Don't run away
I'm reaching for you.
Please come
Boldly enter in.

The Cleansing

Word of God
You cleanse my soul
So I can walk with You
Not in part, but whole.
I seek to walk in Your Glory
To behold the face
Of the one who loves me.

Word became flesh,
You cleanse my life
In You I arise
From a new birth.
I proclaim Your name
And rest in the anointing
Of Your Holy hands.

Word of God
You are the Way
You are the truth
And You are the light.
You bless me with
A cup that overflows
To win lost souls to Your life.

The Commission

I hand you a torch to make it through
    the darkest night that falls.
Hold tight – don't ease your grasp
Hold it high so it can call.
Steady your step in the boundaries of the track
So you won't be disqualified.
Carry this torch into every darkness that you find.
Seek out those who have lost their way
I will not leave you in the darkness
The Lord doth say.
When in doubt, bow and pray!
You shall always pass through
Just be still and know the trials therein
Are my mysteries
And will purify your soul
If you allow it.
Only one word of warning before you go
Many who have gone before
Have lost their way
And by surrendering their torch – have gone astray.
Don't ease your grip, I say.
Watch out for fear and doubt.
They will surely attempt to cramp your arms and legs.
There will be days when you feel faint.
Pride and despair at your torch will snare,
But in all of this remember
Your faith in Me will sustain you there.
The journey will seem long and difficult at times
But if you abide in My will,
You'll return to Me,
A Son.

The Dance

Can you imagine dancing with the Lord
led in perfect timing
securely in His arms
Lifting you off your feet
smoother than a figure skater
Just like the wind does a leaf?

O Dear Jesus
       sweep me off my feet today
       lift me even higher in You
       than I've ever been before
O how I long to dance with You
       Like the eagle soars.

O Lord send
       Your Holy Spirit wind
       Breathe into me as You descend
Jesus my desire is to be one with You
Thank you for Your Word
       And for making me new.

Release me from all apprehension
of what others may think of me
Fill me with Your compassion
       for everyone I meet
So that I may see them
       even as You see me.

Holy Spirit of Jehovah
       I hear You coming
       as a mighty rushing wind
I see and hear Your might and power
Bringing coals from the altar
       To cleanse those willing to be sent.

Yes Jesus, You may have
　　my life as a dance
May I be as an autumn leaf flying
　　where You will and when
I will dance with You my Jesus
　　Until You come again.

Nothing now to tie me
　　to the world in which I live
You, O Lord, set me free
　　from all shame and sin
I will wait here for You, until I feel the lifting
　　of us dancing off in the Wind.

Chorus:
Come now Holy Fire
Purify my heart again
This world I live in
Is so full of sin.
Cleanse, guide, equip me
To fulfill Your will
Let there be nothing
keeping me from being still
while I wait for the dance.

The Dive

In deceitful silence
The weapon is drawn
And visibly succumbs to fog.
Once entrapped,
NO ESCAPE
Injury and havoc, the solemn fate
Of those lost in blindness.
On a collision course
Confusion descends;
Death's curse
That mystical phenomenon
Swallows its prey.
Only those of the Miracle saved.
The lost, no longer subject to this worldly fate,
Are grievously mourned by those
The mist did not take.

The Dwelling

Lord there's a place
Inside my heart
That only You can satisfy
No other heavenly thing
Or on earth can fill
This place for only You.

Not wealth
Not power
Not recognition or pride
Can rule my heart in peace and love
Like Your dwelling inside.

There are lusts of this world
Seeking to invade
This holy place You call home
But cheap imitations
Leave me all alone
But You, O Lord, are mighty
To the pulling down of these strongholds.

And no wealth
No power
No recognition or pride
Can rule my heart in peace and love
Like Your dwelling inside.

The Father's View

I have a home
In the valley by a stream
Where wild game passes
Beneath pine trees
Amidst wildflowers
And blade of grass
A place where beauty is unsurpassed.

I have a home
In the mountains
High above the clouds
Where the storms pass under
And I can surround
All of creation beneath My eye
A place so bright no one can see with naked eyes.

I have a home
In creatures below
When they open their heart to Me
Though I am in Heaven
Where angels sing praise
My home extends throughout the universe
For I am the Creator,

I AM, YAHWEH.

The Gathering

In Your love
You sent Your Son to us
So we who never knew You
Could become
The children of God.

Burn now Your flame within
The Holy Spirit kindling
The Good News
You sent to men…
Complete redemption.

Broken from the curse
Let us shout hallelujah again
And dance around
In Your glorious love
A precious child of God.

Created, not evolved
In the image and likeness of our God
We long for the day
When we shall be One
Just as You prayed in the Garden.

Burn now Your flame within
The Holy Spirit kindling
The Good News
You sent to men…
Complete redemption.

The Lamb and the Storm
(Final Chapter)

The bleeding one lies alone
Casualties seen before
     now remembered – become the door
     to resurrect truth
     to be explored.

Knowing the outcome
the bleeding soul cries out
and cannot forget
the pain of the final blow.
The arduous life
now halted
by a seeming mistake
Soon to conclude
the number of His days.

Is it God's wrath
     Or His salvation?
He can hear the enemy proclaim
     the Win
     as He draws near
     with explosives
     at point blank range
Each second of His life
     An
     E—t—e—r—n—i—t—y

Death glares at the soul
      with hate in its eyes
Wishing only to inflict more pain
      before the bleeding soul dies

Fighting for each breath
      He gasps
      Strangled by the blood
      The very blood lost
      Which claims His life;
Salvation for our souls.

The suffering, once an evil prison
Which was thought to have ended all hope
Cries VICTORY as He dies,
Shining Salvation's light
Eternally defeating the foe.

The Mask

I've worn a mask
most of my life
to hide my identity
But when my eyes saw Jesus
I wanted to know He saw me...
and not the mask
I used to cover
the mud and tear streaked face.
I wanted Him to see the tears
the red burning eyes
the blemishes
and clogged pores
infected from bacteria
and neglect.
He said he couldn't heal
what I didn't expose
and I had to believe
"According to your faith
may you be healed,"
I heard Him say.
No Lord, I replied
First heal my faith...
It lacks so...
I've not enough
To faithfully follow...

With tears and brokenness I begged
Lord make me new
Please clean the mess I've made
I'm trapped in a
transparent prison
that only You can see.

Lord Jesus, please
I know that You are
the only one
who can set me free.
"Do you trust Me?" He asked.
Yes Lord, I replied.

"Then you know
what I have is yours
if you shall ask,"
said He, as He removed the mask...

Please give me the faith
I need for You to be pleased.
I want to do whatever it takes
so I'll need endurance for this race.
Lord I confess all my sins
I give You all I know
And I'll come back to confess even more
If you will teach me Your ways.
I want to be like You Lord
From now through the rest of my days.

And He touched my blind eyes with spittle
To dry my endless tears
And filled my heart with a love
Far greater than my fears.
He forgave my sins
He made me new
In such a way
That's a mystery.
And I know beyond all doubt
Only God Himself
Can restore
The leper's unclean sores.

Praise flows from my heart today
Once in chains
Now I'm free…
Once a tare
Now a Harvest seed…
Once a hidden leper,
Now I'm clean…
Once forbidden –
Now Redeemed!!!

The Path

Proverbs 3:5-6   Psalms 121:3   Hosea 4:1-11

The world is our path
and in this world we know
both day and night
before we are very old.
In church we learn
that God is the Lord of light
and Satan, the evil one
seeks darkness for his play.
Living is traveling
the paths we cross everyday
even losing our direction
getting lost along the way.
Journeyers soon learn
to advance during light
to use the path markers
not visible at night.
At night the wise man seeks
rest for his head
awaiting the return
of the morning light again.
He knows of the evil
that lurks in darkness
and sets up watch
that he not be ambushed
before first light.
He pitches his shelter
eats and rests by his fire.
He has planned his journey
and stores his trash away
lest thieves and beasts ravage
while he sleeps.

The wise man travels lightly
so he can move expediently
free of excess burden
that would steal his energy.
At first light, he gathers
continuing on his way
until he reaches
the destiny that waits.

But the foolish man heeds not
the warning of the dark's iniquity
traveling onward into dim lit weeds
becoming more lost
than even he is aware;
confusion descends as fog
without the light there.
And once surrounded by the Darkness
he doesn't
know where
he is
AND
Veers off course so easily
He cannot see
when he's circled and returns
to the place he was before.
This foolish traveler of night
seldom rests his head
and when he does
so frequently
it's when light is overhead.
Slumbering by day
he wastes knowledge found in Light
This man is ambushed without mercy
ravaged by hungry wolves
then left for dead
And lest a man's light
crosses the foolish man's path
There is but dim hope in the moonlight
for him to rest
Yet it shines upon him.
It shines upon him
And he does have a chance
With the Morning Light.

The Proclamation

Psalm 19:1: The skies announce what He has done...

I have no control of the winds
in the heavens above
the sunlight or the stars
shining brilliantly thereof.
I've no control of the tides in seas
the currents or the swells
the moon's gravitational pull
on the tides high or low.
I've no control of the atmosphere
whether of earth or beyond
the rains, frosts, or snows
the seasons or day and night.
I cannot create the blood
flowing through my veins
the sap in tree trunks
or crop of sugar cane.
I cannot predict raging river floods
or loss of life
world starvation
or man's waging war.
I cannot create a majestic mountainside
draped in wild flower buds
or know when winter
will blanket it with snow.
I've no power over changing seasons
or the quails mating call
these are all mysteries to me
of which I stand in AWE.

Why do you come and ask for signs of Him
questioning if He is real?
You ask me where I see Him,
yet refute my evidence.
Your anger and defensiveness tell me
you just don't understand
so I offer no further reply
for there is nothing else to say
if these evidences you deny.

So I refuse to speak
and gaze up into the skies
knowing no words can say
what I behold with my eyes.
And my spirit prays silently for wisdom
as you reject what I reveal
and I see dancing synchronicity
the duality of truth and lies
the majesty of Almighty God
and the deceiver of our eyes.
For what greater witness be
than the purity of these
with no agenda of their own?
Where else is His vastness...peace...or majesty?
And from my spirit I reply
Two simple questions I ask:
Are the earth and skies themselves
more faithful and knowledgeable than I?
Existing since creation,
has the universe in which we trod
ever created or believed,
the truth and lies we deny?

The Prophet

I sought the prophet
    not for a sign
        but for healing
        from the Divine.
When He touched my eyes
    the scales sloughed away
        and the darkness of the cave vanished
        as if a stone rolled away.
Then He touched my ears
    deafened from shame
        and I heard angels singing
        comfort to me
in the Lord's Name.
He stroked my hair
    dancing in the wind
        and told me of their counting
        which the Lord told him.
He seared my tongue
    with coals of fire
        and it no longer spoke
        of its own desires.
He raised my bowed head
    prostrate from the fall
        and instilled in me the courage
        to escape prison walls.
He caressed my hands
    and showed me the holes
        the Savior bore
        to preserve my soul.
He straightened my bones
    so upright I stand
        no longer condemned
        on shifting sand.

He removed my shoes
        to wash my feet
                and blessed them too,
                that they should lead.

New birth yet laboring
        in a deep sleep I fell
                and beheld dreams
                of Heaven and Hell.
The infant head crowning
        I saw the birth of the Son
                and heard angels singing
                glorious praises above.
Then just before birth
        I heard the prophet say
                "The Lord is renewing minds
                that seek His way."
When I opened my eyes
        no prophet I saw
                yet my eyes beheld the glory
                of the Lord fulfilling the Law.
I rose to follow after Him
        when I heard Him say,
                "This place He has prepared for you,
                you can now walk in His strength."
"There's yet another home
        He's preparing for you
                and when He returns He will gather
                Those who have proclaimed His truth."
I blinked my eyes
        and He vanished
                yet, I knew He had been there
                for I was clothed in the armor, I had
                seen Him wear.

Amazed at my new being
        I studied every inch
                my heart no longer aching
                no more filth or stench!

Running, leaping and praising God
  I vowed He could send me as He wished
    and with my rejuvenated soul I sang
      glorify Jehovah, who made me whole!
What a wonder to me
  that I should receive such a precious gift
    as His love for me!

The River

Come and cleanse me like a virgin river
Come and wash away my unbelief
Set me free from all that keeps me
Bound in sin and shame.
Come and cleanse me like a virgin river
Flood my soul today
Uproot me and carry me away!
Flow through me mighty river
Until I'm free again.
Wash and empty my vessel
Until no more I am.
Fill me with Your Holy Spirit
So my heart and my words
Flow into others
With the power and compassion
Of the Lion and the Lamb.

The Silence

Meditations: II Chronicles 7:14; Proverbs 28:13;
I Peter 2:11; Galatians 5:16-21;
James 4:1-6

Hello Darkness, Secret's friend
I've come to bury my conscience again
It convicts and causes pain
So I must not let it reign
Would a just God bring such
      misery guilt and shame?
I doubt the claim
And demand the Silence.

Many times I've traveled this road
Burying sins untold...
'Til I no longer regret
I go my own way and forget.
But in forgetting
      I am left all alone...
No more conscience to guide my soul
I sit alone in Silence.

In the Silence, no utterance of prayer
And there's no peace anywhere...
Each moment splinters away
Unconnected to its day.
And tomorrow fragments
      before it ever begins...
While yesterday doesn't exist
In this world of Silence.

Many come here - few escape…
Less often now, I ponder their fate
It seems such a futile game
Searching for the hidden things.
And all the values
       I once held so dear…
Have no place here
In unrepented Silence.

In the Silence, I sit and cry
Finding I have bought a lie…
That in hiding, nothing was concealed
And to God all was revealed.
Why did I refuse
       the faith, acceptance and love
The Father's very Dove
That could have overcome – the Silence?

The Surrendered Stone

Meditations:
John 8:4-11
Romans 2:1-4
Matthew 7:1-5
Matthew 5:7-8

How can I condemn my brother for the fault I see
Change the circumstances and it could be me.
Another place and time I was the same
Caught in charade I wanted no part,
Feet shackled and struggling to be released
In human heart I lacked strength and relief.

Do I believe I have the answers
Or do I seek wisdom greater than my own?
Lest I forget the sanctity of my soul….
Do I debase my guard and flee in retreat
Grasping for possessions to lie at my feet?
Or discern with caution against evils unseen?

Fog settles over the river before the dawn
And with the warmth it begins to rise.
No my brother, I cannot condemn;
For I see in your face, places I have been.
And I hear my spirit say,
But for the grace of God go I.

The Testimony

The howling wind calls to the trees
It tells them when to bud and bear new leaves
To extend its branches to Heaven above
To reach out and shelter the dove
To turn green in the spring
To provide a seat for birds that sing.

The gentle breeze calls to the flower
Telling it to open in the morning hour
To spread its joy to the world
For it is a pearl
Bending without breaking in the wind
They are without a single sin.

The water calls to the riverbed below
Steering it in the direction to flow
Take mankind and lead them forward
To see the seagull soar
Warn the banks of the Springtime flood
Prepare for the upcoming mud.

Ocean trade wind, vast as you may be
Take the ships safely over the sea.
Warn us of rising storms,
Assure us on days so warm.
O God, forever be the horizon
Of my rising and setting sun
And I long that in me,
Thy will be done.

The Worm

Meditations: Psalms 49:15; 53:5;
I Corinthians 12:12-13, Revelation 22:5

The worm creeps slowly toward the surface
A slow
Journey
With no
Great gains
Only slow
Consistency...
The depth profound
The earth surrounding...
dark
And cold
Sometimes wet
Muddy or mushy
And other times
Solid
As
Clay
Or
Unyielding
As
Granite...
Yet
With perseverance
The surface is...B—R—O—K—E—N
Even without eyes,
The creature knows His striving has not been in vain
As the beaming warmth penetrates its body.
The journey behind, the task finished
Now only a memory
For a new purpose unveils.
The great purpose...the reason for its very existence...
A self-sacrifice of life
For the continuance of life itself.

Throne of Grace

I come to Your throne of grace this morning
To lay all of my burdens down,
In my flesh I'm feeble and weary
Without Your strength I will surely fail.

Each time I fall it leaves another injury
The wound heals but the scar never goes away.
Lord, You know my wounds are many
Because I've failed first to come and pray.

Forgive my stubborn independence
Which leads me down the road to fail.
Teach me now to call Your Holy Spirit
To trust You long before the gale.

No more deep valleys full of sinking sand
You hold for me the Promised Land.
You assure to bring me through this place
When I put myself in Your Mighty Hands.

I have tasted the trust this world offers
So tempting yet so bitter of an end.
My only hope is to leave it all
Surrendered at Your feet.

So I come to Your throne of grace this evening
Having laid all of my burdens down,
Comforted knowing I'm not defeated
But with You shouts of Victory prevail!

Throne of Mercy and Grace

Meditations: Psalms 25; 45:6-7; Isaiah 6:1, 66:1;
Hebrews 1:8; Revelation 3:21

To You, O Lord
I lift my soul
O my God
I trust in You.
I will not be ashamed,
Because I've set my eyes
On Your throne of mercy and grace.

Your throne of mercy and grace
Is forever and ever.
Your righteousness
anoints and heals as oil.
Heaven is Your throne
the earth Your footstool
And yet You bid me to come.

Show me Your ways
Teach me Your paths
Lead me in Your Spirit and truth
For You are the God
Of my salvation
For You I wait on bended knee.

I remember
Your tender mercies
And know Your loving kindness
is forevermore.
You beckoned me, yet a sinner
And pardoned all iniquity
So I lift my voice
To praise Thee!

Thy Kingdom Come

Lord I speak oneness and prosperity
For each earthen vessel of man.
And in Your church
Let Your river flow.
May Your will
Flood earth as in Heaven
The source unending
All that was, is and will be.

Place in our hearts
Songs of honor and glory.
Our praise, a sacrifice
Aroma pleasing to Thee,
Rounding Your throne
Where Elders and angels sing
"Arise O Man
Worship Your King!"

Title Medley

A stormy night
A ship at sea
Searches for light
Lost at sea

Tossed to and fro
Water breaking the rail
Darkness long
The Captain wails

The crew weary and exhausted
Weak from work and wave
Grasping tightly to whatever anchored
As they are thrown past

Grasping and failing
The wind and waves take their toll
The Captain praying
Voice shivering in the cold

"God save us!" he shouts.
His skills not enough
The crew fainting
In waters rough

Alone at the helm
The Captain cries
"God take me quickly
Lest in this tide I die!"

Just then a faint sound
From the nameless shore
A foghorn wailing
And a beacon warns

Angry seas unforgiving
Throw the ship on the rocks
The Captain and crew overboard
The ship is lost

Cold and senses failing
Bowing their heads to die
Safety lines fall
From what seems to be the sky.

Amazed and bewildered
They reach for the line
Plucked from the sea
To a safe haven nearby

Night, then day passes
Now warm and dry on shore
The Captain awakens to thank
The saver of his soul

As he looks around him
To his left, then right
No one but his crew present
The horn and beacon light

Each man arises
To await the rescue
And begins singing
Amazing Grace

Favorite songs a singing
Each their testimony be
The song they remembered on page 403
The hymn: Love Lifted Me

Then the Master of the sea
Heard my despairing cry
And from the water lifted me
Now safe am I

Amazing Grace
My song shall ever be
How great Thou art
Love lifted me

Rock of ages
O to be like Thee
Take my life and let it be
Whiter than snow

Covered by the blood
He brought me out
Glorious freedom
He leadeth me

Eternal Father, strong to save
I would not be denied
My anchor holds
Blest be the tie that binds

I am resolved
I'd rather have Jesus
I will sing the wondrous story
Of my Savior's love.

<u>To Him</u>

To Him that dwelleth in the secret place
of the God Most High
Praise from my lips doth rise,
To bless Thy Name both night and day
Knowing Your light leads eternally,
That without You my soul would be lost
By the frill and folly of my own hand.

But praises I sing: I've seen Your light
And there's a luminous glow in every darkness of night.
I know You see my every tear
And likewise hear my every prayer,
As I thank You for the wisdom You unfold,
I ask for You to incline me to do as I'm told.
To be faithful and obedient
Even when I don't understand
The mysteries of Thy hand
And know I can always see Your face
If I will bend my knee.
And whenever I hear You say what is Your will for me
Yet in my heart I fear and plea:
"Lord, you're asking me to be someone I don't know,"
Remind and charge me softly with Your still small voice
"Only like Jesus…with raiment white as snow."

Today and Eternity

My heart can be unyielding
or on bended knee
as I sit comfortably in the pew
every Sunday and Wednesday eve.
So preacher man I ask you
How do you know
if my heart is tender
or bitter cold?
He looked into my eyes
as if to see my soul
and answered the question
I had pondered so.
If you have sold your heart
your eyes will see
yet your spiritual eyes will be blind;
and you will be a deaf mute
in your prayer life
And just as an impaired driver
in the night
you will veer to the left and then to the right.
Your life will lose its meaning
and purpose divine;
while you go through motions
with robotic design.
And while he spoke
I knew he would know
if my actions revealed
a heart grown cold.
Because with God's Spirit
man can see
both today
and future.
With perked ears he can hear
and carefully discern
the lies of the spirits
and truth spoken by the Word.

Transformation

Jesus rose from the dead
To intercede on behalf of men
Take the seed
Seal it in
It will die
Then grow toward light
Even though we don't understand

More beautiful
In perfect light
Reaching to the heavens bright
Graceful fragrance
Ever sing
Light of glory
Transforming me.

Trinity Song

Father, Creator
Almighty, Omnipotent
El Shaddia, Jehovah
Eloheim, Omniscient
Jehovah Shammah
Nissi and Jireh, too
Triune God,
Holy Father
Abide in me and purify.

Holy Spirit
Gentle and kind
Unquenchable Fire
Comforter of mine
Burn in my heart
Words of truth
Mature me
So I am pleasing
To You.

Jesus, Son of God
True lover of my soul
Ever burning ember
Fiery eyes of Holy love
My righteousness of God in Christ
He who washed me so I am
A Holy spotless bride.

United Front

Hear now the Spirit speak,
"Unity among the people of God."
O Spirit of gentleness,
Brush our lips
as You pass by
Indwell our hearts
with Your burning embers!
Dance all of you who praise the Lord!!
Sing and praise Him
all you of Zion
city on a hill.
He who has an ear
Let him hear!
Behold how good
And how pleasant it is
For brothers to dwell together
In Unity!

Vision of Grace

The fog descended and rose again
With my eyes opened I saw the Eternal's flame
Consuming my sin as ash…
    The weakness of my frame.

      I bowed in vain worshipping idols
          while bound in fetters and chains.
      I'd seen them before
        as earthly pleasures;
        never as pain
        but now…undeniably
        blood guilty stains.
In the vision
    my heart cried out in grief
    and condemning shame.
Tears flooded my eyes
    as I longed to be free
    as before the time of my birth.
I see it now as the new day's dawn
Living in the presence of the One True God,
In love, fully adorned.

In shame, I hid my face
        pleading for mercy undeserved,
    When as a child He lifted and held me
      near His breast
    And wiped away my tears.
"My child, do not fear," I heard the Savior say.
"I've known your sins since before thy days
    and atoned for every one.
The trial, the stripes, the crown of thorns
    and yes, my death upon that tree
    brought Death to death
    for all who will believe.

Step into the light my child
    surrendering your fear
    and feel now as My last words on the cross
    absorb every tear.
You, my child are fully known
    My statutes now embedded in your soul
    Guard them with all your heart
    and you will never be alone.
When you falter, as you will
    along your earthly path
    rise again and brush the dust from your face
    believe in My power, My love and
    My grace.
Peace to you now, My precious child
Your feet stand restored on the righteous path.
Walk now in the purpose
for which I've called your name,
Declare My words and offer praise.
I AM the Almighty God
Forever Merciful and Unchanged."

Well of God

Rise up
Spring forth
Flow living water
Faithful Spirit
Resurrection power
Rise up in me
Life giving supply.

Deep well
River flowing
Mighty geyser
Gushing forth
Overflowing
Unstoppable power.

You break the dams of captivity
And set Your people free.
You released your love unending
Upon that tree at Calvary.

Teach me to draw
From Your well
To receive Your blessings
Instead of the curses of Hell.
Cleanse my ears
So I can hear You.
Wash my eyes
So I can see.
Pour Your grace
On my hands and feet,
So I can serve you
Faithfully.
O Lord water me
From Your well
To set others free.

We've Come
Meditation: Acts 4:12

Lord we've come to worship
    and praise Your Holy name
For You've forgiven and cleansed us
    of all guilt, sin and shame.
Mighty is Your river
Brilliant Your light
We worship You in truth
There's no darkness in Your light.

We raise our hands to You, Lord
    no other god satisfies.
We praise You for opening
    our ears and our eyes.
Empower us Your people
To go and conquer sin.
Our lips shall not be silent
For Your glory lives within.

When I Think of You

When I think of You
At the Last Supper
And Your betrayer
Dipping in the cup with You
Then in the Garden
The Roman army
And Judas' kiss:

I don't know
How You endured without sin
I just know You did
And it was all for my gain.

When I think of You
Led off like a criminal
Before the Chief Priests
In the middle of the night,
That illegal trial
Insults and mocking
And how You stood there in silence
When at Your word
Angels would have carried You away:

I don't know
How You endured without sin
I just know You did
And it was all for my gain.

Then as if that weren't enough
You stood before
Governor and King
All alone
All those You loved – scattered
The insults and mocking hurling
Knowing what daylight would bring:

I don't know
How You endured without sin
I just know You did
And it was all for my gain.

Then found faultless
Before Pilate and Agrippa
The crowd yelling "Crucify!"
The scourging and spitting
Crown of thorns and purple robe,
The yanking of the hair
Of the very face of God.
Broken and bleeding
Carrying that cross on
Your flesh torn back
Staggering to that shameful hill.

I can almost hear
The hammer pounding still
The nails
Through Your feet and hands
Your heart already broken by man,
Then the piercing pain, too
As they gambled Your clothes away
And God too, turned away His face:

I don't know
How You endured without sin
I just know You did
And it was all for my gain.

And I'll never know the pain
Of the betrayal of all my friends
The crowd's deafening screams
Of the word "Crucify!"
The pain of broken heart
And torn flesh for the sins
Of mankind
And the gasping for air
As Your blood flowed there
At the foot of the cross

As You cried out and died.

And when I think of this horror
That act of faith we know as love
I wonder how as man You endured it;
Yet, I know Your strength came from
The fullness of God in Your heart and soul
The unity of One.

Because of You
My empty cup runs over,
With Your blood
The sacrifice satisfied
By the longing heart of the Father.
God Himself paying the price
For His children to come home
All because…
All because of You.

And that would have been enough
For all our sins to be washed away
Yet You brought us so much more
When after three days
You defeated the grave and rose again
And sent the Comforter
'Til You should come again.

Hallelujah, hallelujah
Hallelujah, sing praise to the Lamb!
Hallelujah, hallelujah
Hallelujah, sing praise
To the Lamb and the King of Glory
For the sacrifice!
Now He reigns forever
And there will be a day He comes again
And we'll join Him in the clouds
And His glory will descend
Then we'll reign with Him forever
Hallelujah to the Lamb!

When the Wind Blows

When the wind blows
Let your anchor hold firm
Grounded in the teachings of His Word
Fastened to the Lord in prayer
So when the wind blows
Your heart remains sincere.

So let the wind blow
I will place my trust in Him
Because He is faithful, time and time again
The Lord my God, I will praise
When the wind blows
And on breezeless days.

Whoever Calls

Whoever calls is healed
Whoever calls is raised
God provides for all our needs
And meets our faith with grace
For them who call on Jesus' name.

Draw near to Him
Dare to seek His face
For even if as a mustard seed
He rewards with unmerited grace
Whoever calls on Jesus' name.

It doesn't matter where you've been
There's no need to hide from Him
He already knows all your sin
And used the power of His blood
To blot them out – each and every one
When we are faithful to call on Jesus' name.

Winter Dawn

You know I've tried and tried
Yet sometimes I just seem to fail
Where will I find the strength
For You to prevail?
Oh Jesus, help me please
To make it through another day
Knowing You will give me strength
If I only pray.

Lord, I'm trusting You
I've no where else to go.
Change my heart
Change all of me if You must
My thoughts and my dreams, too
For me to make it through.

The night is so dark
And I feel so alone
Jesus I am trusting You
To be with me 'til the dawn.

Jesus, I feel I have no right
To ask any favor of You
But have no where else to go
My own strength has failed me so.

I trusted You to forgive me
For my sinful ways
And You picked me up and loved me
And pointed me in the right way.

So with each breath I'm praising You
For listening to my prayers
For just being here.
I'm grateful in heart
And know I'm restored
By the First and Last
Jesus my Lord.
I will love You always
For the rest of my days.

<u>Word of God</u>

Word of God
You cleanse my soul
So I can walk with my God
Not in part
But face to face.

I seek to walk intimately with You
To behold Your glory
Through and through
To behold the face
Of my risen King.

Word of God
You restore my soul
So I can arise
And see with restored sight
Knowing I am loved.

I rest in the presence
Of Your anointing
Your holiness,
Your shining glory
Your mercy and grace.

Word of God, You are the way
Your Holy hands
I seek with my face
The loving hands of power
and warm embrace.

My cup runneth over
With unending love and grace
How can I be silent
With such a love's embrace
Looking upon my Savior's face?

Word of the Lord

Meditation: John 1:1-6

Before men
I will proclaim
The Word of the Lord.
I will keep silent
While He speaks
That I may hear
To perform His perfect will.

Let the Word of the Lord
Be written in my heart.
After He speaks,
I will shout
Lest the rocks
Begin to cry out.

The Word of the Lord goes out
Never returning void.
May this Word
Lead my actions and thoughts
All the days of my life
Now and forevermore.

Hear the shout of victory
Spoken in the Word
Sinners once shackled
Now are free
All because Jesus,
born a man
Spoke, lived, and died
the Word of the Lord.

You Had Mercy

In bondage – all alone
Drowning sorrows in alcohol
Boosting confidence with drugs
Trying to escape it all in suicide;
When another comes along
And doesn't condemn but loves
And he trades shooting up
For the one who dries his tears
And holds him close.
Walking together out of the rain
I hear the new song that he sings:

O Rock of ages
Thou art amazing grace
Nothing but the blood of Jesus
I stand so amazed.
Come fount of every blessing
As I come into the garden alone
O the deep, deep love of Jesus
It is well with my soul!

No more meaningless videos
I've found the wonders of God.
You had mercy on me
In the days of wandering
Swaying and staggering
Unfaithful in my love,
Then seeing my own weakness
And smelling my own stench
I called Your Name
And though faint and wretched
You embraced me
And had mercy on my soul.

Mercy
Mercy on my soul
You had mercy on me
And I'm no longer alone
Mercy
Mercy on my soul
Your life makes me whole.

I look around and see
Those still in bondage
To drugs and alcohol
So many temptations
Lurking to steal us away
Gossip, pride, idolatry
That and more so common place
And I still know too many
Hiding their real face.
And for them I cry:

Mercy
Have mercy upon their souls.
Embrace them Father
So they can be made whole.
I know You hear their cries,
Soften their hearts
So they will cry:
Mercy
Have mercy on my soul.

I see the downcast
Ill and deformed
Where are the Samaritans
To help the unborn??
So many pass by
Without time to care
But there is one who will never err.

Mercy
You had mercy on my soul
Mercy
No longer alone
Mercy
Mercy on my soul
Only Your life
Makes me whole.

Friend look to Jesus
Who has mercy on your soul
Cry to Him in desperation
He forgives and loves,
Never ridicules.
And you too can come
Cleansed and welcomed
Like the prodigal son.
He is waiting
For you to come Home…

Sing with me:
Mercy
Mercy on my soul
Mercy
No longer alone
Mercy
Mercy on my soul
Only Your life
Makes me whole.

Your Name is Holy

In Your Name
There is mercy for sin
There is safety within
In Your Holy Name

In Your Name
There is strength to remain
To endure beyond the pain
Your Name is Holy.

Your Ways, O Lord

Your ways, O Lord –
are higher than my own
And Your thoughts focused
while mine prone to roam.
So my paths
I now leave behind
I will press on
and live with the mind of Christ.

"I send my angel
To witness to you
in the churches,
I am the root
and the harvest
The radiant star
of dusk and dawn."

The Spirit and the Bride say, "Come"
And let him that hears
let him too say, "Come."
Let him that is thirsty rise
and come near.
And whoever will
May drink freely from the river of life.

<u>Yours</u>

A broken and contrite heart
You will find at Your feet.
I stand an empty vessel
Waiting for You to fill me.
I've poured out all I've known
And ever wanted to be.
O Lord, I worship You
I worship You
I worship You
And for You
I will wait.

I will wait for Your blessing.
I am ready to change
Anything I need to
That would get in Your way.
There's just no more room for me
Cause when I'm full
There's no room left for You.
Lord, I worship You
I worship You
I worship You
I am Yours.